Many gardening pleasures and tasks are connected with particular seasons. Some jobs need doing throughout the entire growing season.

W9-CCE-395

SPRING

SUMMER

JOACHIM MAYER

Container Plants for Beginners

▶ ABCs of Plant Care
▶ Choosing Plants for Decks and Patios
▶ Design Suggestions for Every Season

Over 290 Color Photographs
by Friedrich Strauss

Illustrations by Renate Holzner

BARRON'S

Contents

Designing Decks and Patios

Plant Care

Plant Care

Pathways

to Magnificent Bloom

With some know-how about plant maintenance, the entire range of attractive deck flowers, hothouse plants, and ornamental shrubs is at your disposal.

Whether the space is a modest 50-sq. ft. (5-m²) deck or a huge patio, an expansion of an already-existing garden or the only place available for enjoying greenery and a wealth of flowers outdoors—the basic premises for deck gardening vary widely. Common to all situations, however, is the use of plants in pots, planters, and flower boxes. This form of gardening has some special features when it comes to care, but on the other hand, it offers many exciting possibilities for using beautiful plants and creating effective displays with them.

Mobility in the Potted Garden
"Planter or container growing" doesn't sound very exciting, so catchy words like pot gardens or mobile gardens were coined. Here, of course, it is the plants that are "mobile," and in a way you are not able to in the garden, you can site them, move them, and arrange them almost anywhere you want. Even warmth-loving beauties from distant countries that wouldn't last long planted out in the garden can

be kept happy when cultivated in a pot or planter on the deck or patio. You can even keep the plants over the winter in an above-freezing spot in the house or in a heated greenhouse so that they are protected from the assaults of winter.

Beauty Contest on the Deck
"Geraniums" (which, strictly speaking, are called pelargoniums), petunias, and fuchsias have been at the top of the hit parade for decades as beautiful, sturdy, persistent bloomers. But you should keep in mind the wealth of other attractive deck flowers, too. Furthermore, garden plants are increasingly appearing in pots and planters: Perennial plants and the less vigorous growers among the shrubs enrich the selections. They are hardly any more difficult to maintain than the classic deck flowers. Try and make use of the entire multiplicity, even if it seems overwhelming at first. This book will help you to find a negotiable path through the "jungle" of possibilities.

Using different kinds of plant containers opens up many possibilities for beautiful designs.

Good Choices Cut Care in Half

To some degree, the numerous possibilities for planting a deck or patio sort themselves out on their own when you choose plants according to their needs. The better their requirements are fulfilled by the existing conditions, the more the plants will thrive and the less effort will be needed for care and keeping them healthy.

The two most important criteria for choosing are:

▶ The demands of the plant in relation to location factors like light and wind conditions,

▶ Space requirements in respect to space available.

Light and Sun

Happily, decks, balconies, and patios are oriented in every direction—south, west, east, north—which you might think would characterize how much a particular one might benefit from the sun. Certainly the unshaded southern deck receives the most direct sun, the northern deck the least. But don't forget that, even with these simple categorizations, a shading building next door, for instance, or large trees may make the actual direction of the sun of little consequence.

The overwhelming majority of deck flowers like it warm and sunny. This does not mean, however, that you can only avail yourself of the unlimited resources in an unshaded south situation:

▶ In the portraits section (beginning on page 54) you will discover that many beautiful varieties also tolerate shade or part shade.

▶ Even the most sun-loving of plants are happier if placed out of the broiling midday sun in summer. Awnings and similar shading devices offer relief.

▶ Important to know: For plants it is primarily a matter not of sun but light that they need for developing nutrients (photosynthesis). Therefore, some part-shade plants may definitely thrive on a bright, unshaded north deck, even if they don't flower so luxuriantly.

▶ A white-painted wall and white furniture are not only pleasing to look

Ornaments for Shade

In balcony areas that lack sun, fuschias and ferns create interesting accents, as do ivy, hostas, and other attractive foliage plants.

at on a bright, sunless deck, but they also increase the quantity of light available for the plants.

▶ On the other hand, it is very hot in front of a white south-facing wall in summer because of the reflected sunlight. Many plants tolerate this poorly, and the danger of insect colonization increases, especially for potted roses and dwarf conifers.

Wind and Rain

As a rule, it is on the exposed north- and west-facing decks where plants most often suffer from inclement weather. But you should also be aware in other situations and especially on patios open on all sides that some plants may be especially susceptible to wind or rain (see plant portraits starting on page 54). Often such species need a protected little corner to themselves.

▶ If summer rains threaten to spoil the whole flowering show, a temporary umbrella of floating row cover (agricultural fabric) can help (leave a space over the plants) to keep the deck's summer beauty from going down the drain.

▶ Appropriate climbing plants, trained high on a trellis, can serve as a wind and privacy screen. Be careful, however, as they may also cut off the supply of sunshine.

There is room on the smallest deck or balcony when various levels are utilized for plant placement.

Never Enough Space

Even the largest patio is quickly over-crowded when plants with spreading growth habit and large containers are chosen. Before you buy shrubs for planters, also give some thought to the annual growth in height and spread.

Basically, it is essential to bear in mind:

▶ Stands that are too dense and plantings that are too thick result in the plants' mutually affecting one another. Infestations of insects and, in particular, fungus diseases are promoted.

▶ Overcrowding can impair the total visual effect. Read more about this in the section Creating Harmony, Placing Accents (pages 124–125). There you will find tips on clever use of space.

▶ Hothouse or greenhouse plants and other shrubs can only be kept under control with pruning. If they have attained "giant size," you had better look for a suitable substitute or raise offspring from cuttings.

▶ Exotic pot and tender hothouse plants not only need a sunny summer location protected from wind and rain, they also need winter quarters (usually bright and cool).

▶ It's preferable to plant your deck somewhat sparsely at first, rather than too densely. Any empty spots that develop can be filled in with purchase of new plants until late summer.

Buying Plants and Seeds

No question about it, spontaneous purchases are part of the fun of a deck—who can resist the attractive impulse purchase at the garden center? But to achieve a pleasing, lasting total picture, proceeding according to a plan promises the most success: from careful selection down to the purposeful purchase of plants.

Buy or Raise Your Own?

Lushly floriferous summer flowers like petunias or marigolds play the main roles on the deck. Most are annuals, are sown in spring, die with the first frost, and must thus be purchased anew each year.

If you've had little experience with plants up till now, it's advisable at first to buy plants that are already growing, which are not terribly expensive. But if you've been planting a number of flower boxes for a long time, you can figure on growing your own. After all, raising your own plants adds to the fun. Another advantage: You can grow species and varieties that are hard, if not impossible, to find as seedlings.

Keep Your Eyes Open When Buying Plants

Some nurseries and garden centers start offering young plants as early as March. If you have the facilities for growing these in a light, frost-free situation until time to plant them out in the middle of May (or after the last frost in your area), it is economical to buy them, for plants are quite reasonable before the season begins. The same is true of the after-season (generally from about the beginning of June); but of course then the selection is "played out." In general, the begin-

Growing your own is fun and is also cheaper.

ning of May is considered the best time for buying plants.

You can by all means get usable plants in the supermarket or home building supplies stores, too. However, nurseries offer more guarantees of healthy, optimally cared-for plants, as well as expert advice. The mail-order business is also not a bad resource, though of course the plants can't be examined until after they have been delivered. Otherwise it is recom-

mended that the young plants be very thoroughly examined before purchase. Choose only plants
▶ with sturdy growth, good branching, deep green leaves, and—starting in May—with numerous buds starting,
▶ that are unambiguously healthy, that is, showing no signs at all of disease or pest infestation.

Don't Economize on Seeds

Quality seeds come at a price, which as a rule is repaid with good growing experiences. When buying, you should watch primarily for:
▶ undamaged packaging, preferably guaranteed against germination,
▶ packaging date or expiration date of viability of the seeds.

Precise, easily readable notes about length of viability are also a plus, as well as precisely indicated variety and printed instructions for culture, for example whether the seeds must be covered by soil (dark germinators). Make sure that the seed packets are stored in a cool, dry place where they are being sold. Warmth and dampness can affect the seeds, which you must also keep in mind when storing them at home. With proper storage, the seeds of most species will remain viable for 2–3 years or more. You should close used packages as well as possible and then sow the remainder of the seeds in the following year.

In addition to the main seeding season in early summer, there are special seasonal offerings for fall and spring planting.

Seeds of ordinary species and varieties can be found in the supply sources discussed above. Special items, for instance, uncommon annuals, fragrant plants, or seeds of hothouse plants are offered by various specialty suppliers. The best sources for addresses are your local county extension agency and garden magazines, which often have an extensive trade or advertising section (see Resources, page 152).

Buying Tips for Other Plant Groups

Bulbs and corms	▶ Fall planting: Look for fleshy bulbs (not dried out) without rotten spots, etc; ▶ Spring planting of forced bulbs: Choose varieties that can be planted outdoors later (robust, frost-hardy)
Perennials (plants that live more than one or two seasons)	▶ Choose healthy, compact container plants (already potted) ▶ Sometimes may be raised from seed; propagation by cuttings usually easier
Winter-hardy ornamental shrubs and container fruits	▶ Choose healthy container plants ▶ Growing from seed usually difficult; often propagation by cuttings possible
Hothouse plants (wintered over indoors)	▶ Wide price range depending on size and age; younger plants less impressive, but cheaper, besides taking up less space and easier to acclimate ▶ Choose healthy, uniformly grown plants with roots that permeate the root ball ▶ Propagation from seed usually difficult; often propagation by cuttings possible

Growing Your Own Plants

Information in Brief

Materials, Tools

Seeds
Seed flats, covers
Propagating mix
Kitchen sieve
Wooden board
Labels, waterproof marker
Spray bottle

Growing Temperatures

Optimal germination temperatures:
usually 65°–70° F (18°–20° C)

Germinate at about 59° F (15° C):
Cape marigold
Calceolaria
Pot marigold (calendula)
China aster

Need only 59°–64° F (15°–18° C):
Para cress
Argyranthemum
Zinnia

Need 68°–72° F (20°–22° C):
Swan River daisy
Wax begonia
Scarlet sage
Ageratum
Geranium *(Pelargonium)*
(68°–75° F [20°–24° C])
Petunia

Preparing Flats

Shallow flats with removable covers are best for the early culture of annuals, herbs, and vegetables. Very large seeds can also be planted individually or in groups of a few in small pots. Use only special sowing or growing mix. Smooth the upper surface with the little board, lightly compressing the soil. When you are done there should be about ½ in. (1 cm) of space left between the soil surface and the top to allow for watering.

Sowing

Larger seeds can be spaced ½–¾ in. (1–2 cm) apart. Very fine seeds should be scattered as evenly as possible and not too thickly. This is easier if you mix them with a little sand. To be on the safe side, always sow a little more than you expect to be able to use as plants. Label all sowings with the names of the seeds.

Seeds of most deck flowers need 1–3 weeks to germinate. You can figure on the same length of time for starting vegetables and herbs.

Covering—Not Always Necessary

The seeds of many species germinate only when they are not exposed to light. These dark-germinators are sprinkled with the growing mixture, and then a small board is used to lightly press the soil down again. The soil covering should be at least as deep as the seeds are thick, to a maximum of three times the seed thickness. Light-germinators should be left uncovered or be covered with only the very thinnest sifting. Press such seeds in firmly with the board. Notes on light-germinators can be found in the plant portrait section, but you will usually find information about them on the seed packets as well.

After Sowing

The soil mixture is now watered thoroughly and it then should never be allowed to dry out in the weeks that follow (but not kept "soaking wet" either). It's best to use a spray bottle to water. The cover—or use a sheet of glass placed over the flat—protects from evaporation but must be lifted for air as soon as the first tips of seedlings appear. Place the flats in a warm (see Information in Brief), bright but not too sunny spot.

Alternative: Peat Pellets

The peat pellets swell after thorough watering to become several times their original height. Then you insert one seed per pot in the designated opening; press dark-germinators in deep or cover them with soil. Later the little plants can be planted in pots or boxes, peat pot and all. The roots spread through the fine net that usually holds the pots together. Put the peat pots in a flat with drainage holes and a tray; this is the easiest way to maintain moisture without their becoming soggy.

EXPERT TIP
The garden supply stores also offer "minigreenhouses" with bottom heat.

CROSS-REFERENCE
From Seedlings to Young Plants pages 18–19

From Seedlings to Young Plants

Information in Brief

Suitable Transplanting Containers

Propagating flats
Wooden boxes
Multiplant flats with
holes/individual pots at least
2 in. (5 cm) wide
Pots made of plastic, peat
("Jiffy"), or recycled material,
2½–4 in. (6–10 cm)
(Pots of peat and recycled material decay; they can later be
planted with the seedling in
them)

Other Materials/Tools

Seed-starting mix or other
soilless potting mix
Transplanting sticks or small
sticks
Watering can with a fine spray
head

Time Needed

Transplanting a seeding flat:
about 20–30 minutes

When to Transplant

Depending on the plant
species and development,
3–6 weeks after sowing

Seedlings Need Air

As soon as the first green shows in the seeded flat, the cover should be propped up with a small stick or partly removed to permit ventilation. After all the plants have come up, the cover may be removed entirely. At this point don't keep the seedlings so damp anymore; however, the soil mixture should not be allowed to dry out. Now the flat of seedlings must definitely be placed in a bright spot.

Pricking or Thinning Out

This means moving seedlings that are growing too close together. The best time for this is when the first pair of true leaves unfolds over the two seed leaves (which are usually roundish). You can move the seedlings to stand 2–2½ in. (4–5 cm) apart in the flat or transplant them to little individual pots; optimal substrate: special growing mix. A practical tool for carefully loosening roots and lifting them out is a sharpened stick, which is also used to bore the planting holes in the soil of the transplanting container.

Inspect seedlings and young plants regularly for signs of any diseases— and remove ailing plants immediately.

Shortening Roots

If long roots have already formed, careful shortening at the tip is recommended. The roots should never be "squished together" in the new planting hole. Even with shortening, a little injury during transplanting is unavoidable. Of course this inhibits growth at first, but it stimulates the branching of the roots. After inserting the seedling, carefully press the soil down around it and water thoroughly. As a rule, a somewhat cooler location (around 59° F [15° C]) is beneficial.

Pinching Back the Young Plant

In many species, the pinching or cutting back of the growing tips in young plants promotes compact, bushy growth. To do this, shorten the lead shoot of a plant that is already well developed (depending on the species, at about 4 in. [10 cm] in height) about $^3/_4$–1 in. (2–3 cm). This promotes the development of side shoots. The tips of the side shoots can also be shortened again later. This method is particularly recommended with, for example, argyranthemums, snapdragons, heliotropes, busy Lizzie (impatiens), and cupflower.

Hardening Off Young Plants

There can still be late frosts at night through the end of May in many regions. Only after that are most deck plants placed outside, but then they must still—depending on the climate—deal with cold, rain, wind, or glaring sun. Therefore, it is advisable to get the plants used to their rough life ahead of time. Even on mild April days you can place them outdoors for a few hours. Choose a lightly shaded place that is somewhat protected from the wind.

EXPERT TIP
Pinching back is also recommended for cuttings.

Propagation by Cuttings and Division

Information in Brief

Material/Tools for Taking Cuttings

Sharp knife
3–5-in. (8–12-cm) pots
Growing mix (potting soil and perlite)
Rooting hormone (optional)
Cover of plastic bag, large preserve jar, or other to retain moisture

Materials/Tools for Division

Garden knife
Spade for separating sturdy roots
New pots, depending on plant size
Flower or single-purpose soil

When

For cuttings:

Herbaceous plants preferably in late summer/early fall

Woody plants usually in fall

Hothouse plants in spring, summer

Division:

In spring

Taking Cuttings

Cuttings (here oleander) are best taken from the middle to the end of August. To do it, cut a 2–4-in.- (5–10-cm-) long growing tip from the lead or side shoots (end cuttings) with 4–5 leaves. Make the cut on the diagonal and just below a leaf bud (bulge). The growing tip should not be allowed to bloom; any existing flower buds should be carefully broken off.

Planting Cuttings

Plant a single cutting in a pot filled with a 1 : 1 mixture of potting soil and perlite. Put in just enough mix to leave about a ¼-in. (1-cm) space free at the top of the pot. Before planting remove the two lowest leaves and push the stem ¾–1 in. (2–3 cm) deep into the propagating mix. First dipping the cut surface into rooting hormone powder (garden supply store) promotes root development. Afterwards lightly press the mix down around the cutting and water carefully.

Only take cuttings from mother plants that are healthy, vigorous, and bloom heavily.

Care of Cuttings

It's essential to provide the cuttings with a cover to retain moisture, for example, with a special glass bell (see picture) or a plastic bag that is stretched over the pot on a wire frame. The potting mix should not be allowed either to dry out or to become soggy. Choose a bright, warm spot without direct sunlight. Herbaceous cuttings often root after 2–4 weeks. As soon as new, tender green leaves indicate successful rooting, you must ventilate them and finally remove the cover entirely.

Rooting in Water

Propagation with cuttings is particularly easy with species that root well in water, for example, impatiens, coleus, datura (see picture), oleander. Glasses are suitable—do not use metal containers.

The cut surface of the cutting should be 1–2 in. (3–5 cm) below the surface of the water. As soon as roots have formed, the cuttings are planted in pots with soil.

Propagation by Division

Division is a simple way to propagate perennial plants that put out new shoots from the rootstock. These are primarily potted perennials such as campanulas and astilbes, perennial herbs such as chives, as well as some, such as lily of the Nile (*Agapanthus*, see picture) and bamboos. To divide, remove the plant from the pot and divide the root ball by carefully pulling it apart, with the help of a knife or a spade if the roots are tightly intertwined. Plant the sections in new pots and water thoroughly.

EXPERT TIP
Pot in soil early; long water roots become fragile.

Planting Containers

From a suitable container through the right soil to the proper placement—the planting is the critical step toward long-lasting pleasure in a deck.

In many garden catalogs, planting containers of the most various sorts fill almost as many pages as the offerings of plants for the deck. No wonder, for they share two important functions:
▶ As containers for roots, soil, and nutrients, they make possible any plant life at all on the deck and patio;
▶ as prominent, often decorative elements they contribute much to the total picture of the planting.

Plant Containers for Every Taste

These plant container functions also determine their most important qualifications. Simply put: They should be beautiful, appropriate for the plants, and practical (and moreover, reasonable). There is more on the practical aspects in the next few pages. The "beautiful" is primarily a matter of taste; one person prefers a rustic wooden planter, the next may be most comfortable with colorfully painted concrete planters. The only caution is against too wild a mixture of materials

and colors. On the other hand, there is special harmony created when both the planting and choice of containers lean toward a particular style. A perfect example of such successful harmonizing is a Mediterranean design with deck and hothouse plants in terra-cotta boxes and pots.

The Soil Does It

Much more important for the plants than the container are its contents: the potting soil, also called soilless mix because it is not regular outdoor soil. The plants anchor themselves in it with their roots, they draw nutrients and water from it—those most important prerequisites for healthy growth, good green color, and a profusion of flowers as a result. Here the small amount of soil in the box or pot has to replace the soil of the garden, in which the roots can spread much more widely to take advantage of as many "soil reserves" as possible. So it follows that the potting soil is the last thing on which you should economize.

Pots, boxes, tubs, hanging pots—not only are plant containers holders, they are also design elements.

Of Boxes, Planters, and Pots

One thing should be noted first: In general, you can start with standard flower boxes and clay pots in usual sizes and hardly go wrong buying them. But with time and increasing knowledge of the numerous possibilities, the desire to beautify the deck or balcony with unusual plants and unusual containers is apt to grow. At that time, at the very latest, it's advisable to give some thought to the choice of containers.

Basics of Selection

Whether flower boxes, planters, or troughs—the following criteria are important:

▶ Drainage holes in the bottom of the container are a must, to allow the surplus water to run off—except in the case of the water garden. The holes prevent sogginess and root rot.

▶ Size: Naturally a small plant doesn't need a gigantic pot—still, the fundamental principle applies: the more room the roots have and the more soil that is available to them, the better. Limiting factors are the space available and the weight of large containers.

▶ Heavy containers are more stable, but it's essential to take into consideration the weight-bearing capacity of deck or balcony railings and floors.

▶ Weather resistance saves money in the long run. Containers that are to shelter plants that winter over outside absolutely must be frost-proof.

Materials

There is a wide range of different container materials to consider:
Water is delivered by a siphon bulb from a water storage space separated by a fulse bottom

▶ Plastic containers are light and inexpensive. Durability and proof against frost depend very much on the quality of the plastic.

▶ Earthenware pots are obviously heavier. Their fine pores permit a beneficial exchange of air in the root region. But for the same reason, the moisture can evaporate through the walls, and the outside becomes

Boxes with Water Reservoirs
Water is delivered by a siphon bulb from a water storage space separated by a false bottom.

covered with white calicification. Additional disadvantages: They are breakable and also, in the smaller sizes, they are not frost-proof.

▶ Terra-cotta containers in the higher price categories are thrown and fired especially carefully; cheap versions often differ from ordinary clay pots only in their decoration. Inexpensive alternatives are glazed pots in various colors.

▶ Wooden containers are moderately heavy, frost-proof, and not necessarily expensive. You need a protective coating that is nontoxic to plants, and it must be renewed from time to time. It's best if you set them off the ground on bricks or a grate to prevent rotting on the bottom.

▶ Cement containers (fibrated cement)—now asbestos-free—are relatively heavy, breathe well, are frost-proof and inexpensive, but they are susceptible to breakage. They can be colorfully painted with nontoxic paint.

▶ Metal containers can release substances that are toxic to plants. They must therefore have an inner lining or be lined with a layer of plastic sheeting.

Plant Containers for Every Purpose

There are various different shapes of plant containers to choose from, depending on the intended planting and location of the display or mode of in-stallation:

► There are flower boxes of various materials, colors, and sizes, in lengths between 18 and 48 in. (50 and 120 cm). They should be at least 6 in. (15 cm) high; 8–9 in. (20–22 cm) across allows an optimal planting (arrangements of two or three rows).

► Also, saucer planters should be at least 6 in. (15 cm) deep in the center, and even better would be 8 in. (20 cm), to guarantee good plant growth.

► Hanging pots usually combine a plastic pot with a metal hanger. Besides ceiling and wall mounts there are special arrangements available for attaching them to drain pipes.

► Hanging baskets consist of sheathed wire or plastic, lined with sphagnum or peat moss. The large-meshed baskets can be attractively planted all over.

► Planters are usually nothing more than large pots, but they can also be square or rectangular in shape. For making a choice, besides taste, weight and—in the case of winter-hardy plants like the woody ones—the question of frost-resistance are most important. Large construction pails or tubs with handles for carrying make very practical planters.

► Plant troughs are often rectangular and—unlike pot planters—usually accommodate several plants. On the

Decorative plant containers enrich any deck and any patio—as long as they are practical and suitable for plants.

deck, only plastic or wood can be considered for such large containers. For a permanent spot on the patio, stone or cement troughs are additional possibilities.

Containers with Water Reservoirs

More and more often, containers with water reservoirs are becoming available, not only flower boxes but also other types. The water storage area is separated from the planting area by a partition in the bottom. It is filled through a filler inlet and then gives up the water to the plant roots by means of a siphon bulb or plate in measured amounts. The storage volumes range between 2 and 3 quarts (liters) for 20-in. (50-cm) pots up to 8 quarts (8 L) for 39-in.- (1-m-) sized boxes. Such a water reserve lasts for a few days, but it would not be sure to extend over a longer absence, such as a vacation in midsummer.

When buying, look for
► as stable a construction as possible (for example, with reinforcing supports),
► the presence of a water-level indicator,
► overflow openings or devices in the water reservoir.

Container Preparation and Planting Mix

Before being filled with soil, the planting container should be prepared as well as possible:

▶ Make drainage holes if they don't exist already. Carefully poke through the recesses in the undersides of plastic or clay containers.

▶ Soak clay and terra-cotta containers in water for 1–2 days (for instance, in the bathtub or basement wash sink) before planting, or they will draw too much water out of the soil mix after being planted.

▶ Clean used containers thoroughly with hot water, brush, a little bleach, and soft soap. Scrub off any calcification with vinegar water (do not heat!).

▶ For containers with water reservoirs, also clean between the two bottoms. If necessary, remove any particles of soil or calcium deposits from the opening of the siphoning bulb.

▶ Install drainage for good water flow. This can be shards of old flowerpots, pebbles, or perlite. At least cover the drainage hole, but better still, cover the entire bottom of the container.

▶ In flower boxes, water-conserving moisture mats can also be installed on the very bottom. These siphon off excess water and gradually give it up to the roots.

The Right Planting Mixture

The soil in the plant container should
▶ be able to retain water and nutrients, gradually make them available to the plants, and provide good drainage for excess water,

Soils containing peat (front) are increasingly being replaced by peat-free alternatives.

▶ offer the roots good support, but still remain loose,
▶ be able to moderate extreme wetness as well as temperature swings to some degree. And all this for at least the length of one summer.

Thus it's clear that "any old" flower or garden soil is not necessarily suitable. Put great emphasis on quality potting soil or appropriate soil for container flowers. Also, the so-called "single-purpose soils" (called "type T" or "potting soils") are good. High-quality single-purpose soils are recommended for hothouse plants and potted shrubs. The intermixture of sand (sharp sand—not beach sand—about a quarter of the volume) is often beneficial with such plants. A measure of rock phosphate (garden center), which is carefully mixed in, is beneficial for all plants and soil mixes.

Soil Mixes for Special Needs

As a general rule, a good potting soil mix will be fine for almost all kinds of plants. There are also water-retaining soil mixtures or additives available. Water-storing polymer crystals help keep soil moisture levels higher than regular mixes. These are available at most garden supply stores and through catalogs.

▶ Exceptions are rhododendrons, azaleas, heaths (ericas), and other plants that do not tolerate lime and need acid soil (with low pH value). In these cases you should try to use rhododendron or azalea soil.

▶ It is best to use regular garden soil for planting water plants.

Peat-free Alternatives

Normal flower and single-purpose soils have a high peat content. This substance is almost unsurpassed in

An appropriate soil mix of good quality is an absolute necessity for healthy growth and luxuriant bloom.

its positive qualities (structure, water retention, low salt content). There is one disadvantage that must be taken into account with use of peat substrates: Once it dries out, the substrate can only be remoistened with great effort (such as by placing the entire pot in water). However, the reason for the search for peat-free alternatives is the destruction of the moorlands that results from the stripping of the peat. Even if each deck owner buys only a few little bags full—when added up it comes to many tons annually. Meanwhile, a number of substitutes, often in various mixtures, have proved themselves with testing: coconut fibers, excelsior, bark humus (max. 40% of mixture), and composted green matter (max. 30% of mixture). Also, when buying peat-free mixes, look for quality products that are designated with the appropriate seal of approval.

In addition, keep in mind:
► Water retention is less with substitutes than with peat soils; they must therefore be watered more often and in smaller amounts.
► These peat-free mixes are not suitable for sowing and propagation of cuttings.
► They are also not recommended for rhododendrons, heaths and heathers, fuchsias, begonias, citrus trees, and camellias.

Planting Flower Boxes

Information in Brief

Tools

Trowel
Watering can
Screwdriver or metal gimlet
for poking out drainage
holes

Materials

Flower boxes, as needed
Potting soil, planting mix
Drainage (clay shards, gravel,
or perlite)

Time Needed

20–30 minutes per box

Planting Distances

Large and spreading plants:
8–16 in. (20–40 cm)

Semismall plants:
6–8 in. (15–20 cm)

Small plants:
4–6 in. (10–15 cm)

Placement of Plants

A single-row planting (above, violets and white petunias) is recommended for boxes with less breadth or depth.

If the box is at least 7 in. (18 cm) across, a double-row planting (below) offers a good use of space and beautiful design possibilities: Tall plants (red geraniums) are in the back, semismall plants (marigolds) in the front row, and trailing varieties (lobelia) planted in the "gaps."

Setting Plants In

Fill the box about half full with soil and press it down slightly. Carefully remove the plants from their pots; gently loosen any tightly compacted root balls. First place the larger plants in the center and—when there are arrangements of several rows—beginning at the back. When you are finished, the tops of the root balls should be a good 1 in. (2 cm) below the rim of the flower box.

Don't plant too close together. Any gaps left at first will fill in quickly. If necessary, more plants can always be added later.

Filling in the Soil

After placement of each plant, fill in some soil around it and compress it lightly so the plant is securely anchored. Then fill in the remaining soil, smooth out any unevenness, and press down the surface rather firmly, so that finally there is about 1 in. (2 cm) of room left to the top edge of the box.

Water Thoroughly

Finally, water the soil thoroughly. Water between the plants, which should not get wet at all or only a little. After the first watering, let the upper surface of the soil dry out before you water again. Since the soil will settle with watering, hollows may develop here and there; these should be leveled with additional planting mixture or soil.

After Planting

What looked rather sparse at the beginning (top) displays lush profusion after a few weeks (below). If the plants were not hardened off before planting, the flower box should be placed in a somewhat protected spot without direct midday sun until middle to late May. After about a week the plants will have acclimated themselves well enough to be able to be placed in their "chosen spot." The first fertilizer should be applied 4–6 weeks after planting.

EXPERT TIP
It's best if you water without the spray head attached.

Attaching Plant Containers

Information in Brief

Ways to Attach

Boxes to railings:
> Box brackets with braces preventing tipping, three-part adjustable (for different box heights and widths and railing thicknesses)
> Wire baskets in box form with adjustable holders

Boxes to windowsills:
> Box corner braces, adjustable
> Box supports with screw bolts
> Wire baskets in box shape, screwed in underneath
> Screw hook fastening for wooden boxes

Individual pots:
> Flower pot holders to hang on railings or wire mesh
> Placement in flower boxes

Hanging baskets:
> Ceiling hooks
> Special block and tackle, facilitate care
> Wall brackets

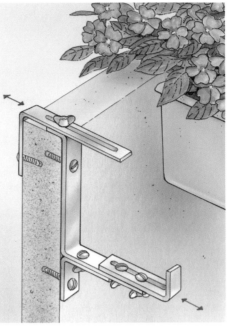

Fastening to Railings

Boxes of any width can be fastened firmly and securely to the deck railing with adjustable brackets. The upper track serves to keep the box from tipping and is standard on good box brackets. Note that sturdy brackets and attaching elements (screws, plugs) are necessary for cement, pottery, and terra-cotta boxes.

Mounts with Corner Brackets

If the box is placed on the window or deck sill, corner brackets are required to prevent slippage forward as well as sideways.

Attachment with Screw Hooks

Hooks screwed into the wall on both sides of the window frame must be well anchored.

Wooden outer boxes into which the hooks are screwed are easy to make; the plants are then planted in plastic boxes inserted into the wooden ones. Sturdy chains can be purchased in hardware and builder's supply stores.

For special attachment problems, it pays to stroll through a builder's supply store. Here you can find many excellent adaptive solutions.

Individual Pots in Flower Boxes

A simple and elegant solution for keeping potted plants from tipping, say, in front of a window or on a deck railing, is to stand them in a box. With this method it's also easier to remove plants that are ailing or that have finished flowering. Quite large pots will fit very comfortably in a box 8–9 in. (20–22 cm) wide and high. You can fill in the space in between with potting soil. It's best to use clay pots. Boxes and holders must, however, hold quite a bit of weight and must be correspondingly sturdy.

Clothing a Wall in Greenery with Wire Mesh

A sturdy, firmly attached mesh of strong wire makes use of a wall as an additional plant surface. Hanging pots and baskets can simply be hung here on hooks and strong rope or chains and be rearranged as desired; there are also special holders for hanging pots. It's best to affix a stout sheet of plastic behind the wire mesh. This prevents damage to the wall from draining water.

Wall Brackets

When there is no way to attach hanging pots or baskets to the ceiling, there are commercially available wall brackets that are often quite decorative. Whether attached to the wall or ceiling, such holders must be "crash-proof." If necessary, exchange the screws supplied with the brackets for longer, stronger screws and plugs.

EXPERT TIP
Wall brackets should be as sturdy as possible and not be too short.

Planting Saucers and Hanging Baskets

Information in Brief

Planting Bulb Pans/Containers

Materials/tools:
Bulb pan, saucer, or other container 12–20 in. (30–50 cm) Ø
Drainage (broken flower pot pieces, gravel, perlite)
Potting soil
Trowel

Time needed:
15–20 minutes per pan

Planting Hanging Baskets

Materials/tools:
Wire or plastic basket with sturdy chain for hanging
Moss (florist supplies) for lining; alternatives: cardboard or sisal lining, coconut matting, felt
Plastic sheeting
Potting soil
Trowel

Time needed:
40–60 minutes

Planting Bulb Pans

First provide the container with a drainage layer $3/4$–1 in. (2–3 cm) deep. In the fall, plant various bulbs in layers according to their species: Put in 1–2 in. (3–5 cm) of soil, place tulips and late-blooming narcissus (always keeping the pointed end up), put in about 2 in. (5 cm) more of soil, then plant the grape hyacinths, crocuses, or early narcissus and again cover with soil—don't forget to leave a space at the top for water. Water gently. Place the potted bulbs in a cool location, as frost-proof as possible, for the winter and do not allow them to dry out.

Adding Spring Flowers

Bulb plantings in small groups produce the most beautiful results, as can be seen here with tulips. Biennial flowers like English daisies, forget-me-nots, and pansies are best added later, in spring. Provide some space for them around the edge of the pot when you are planting the bulbs in the fall.

Plant the flowers carefully so that the bulbs are not disturbed; add some more soil mix and water thoroughly.

A beautiful decorating touch is the hanging basket planted all around to create a complete sphere of flowers.

Preparing Hanging Baskets

For easier working, place the basket in a large pot or pail, or hang it from a strong hook at an appropriate working level. First line entire basket with sphagnum moss or another material (see Information in Brief). Over that goes a layer of sturdy plastic sheeting to keep the soil from trickling out; excess water can drain through a tiny hole cut in the bottom. Fill the basket with as much soil as is needed for the plants planned for the sides.

Planting the Sides of the Basket

For side placement of the plants, first carefully cut slits in the lining material and in the plastic. Thoroughly water the root balls of the plants removed from their little pots. They usually can be threaded into the openings quite easily. It's even easier if you wrap the entire length of the plant in plastic. With the aid of such bags or tubes, the planting goes along without a hitch. Make sure the root ball extends well into the potting soil.

Planting the Top Surface

If you've chosen the "bag" method, you first have to carefully remove the plastic from the side plants. Put in some more soil so that all the roots are well covered. Now the plants on the top surface are so planted that the tops of their root balls come within $3/4$–1 in. (2–3 cm) of the edge of the basket. Fill up to this level with the remaining soil, leaving it slightly higher around the rim to help hold water inside and not spill out. Cut off any plastic sheet that sticks up and finally water thoroughly.

▶ **EXPERT TIP**
Cover the upper surface of the root ball of side-planted plants with moss padding.

▶ **CROSS-REFERENCE**
Hanging Pots and Trailing Plants pages 78–79

Planting Water Gardens

Information in Brief

Suitable Containers

Wooden troughs
Half barrels
Construction drums
(disguised on the outside,
e.g., with wooden palisades)
Pottery and terra-cotta
planters, glazed inside
Metal containers only with
plastic sheeting or waterproof
coating nontoxic to plants
inside

Ways of Leakproofing

Pond lining, 0.8–1.2 mm thick
(with sharp-edged containers,
put padding underneath)
Plastic lining inserts for
wooden troughs (specialty
dealers)
Painting with waterproofing
nontoxic to plants

Other Materials/Equipment

Water-plant baskets
(6–8 in. [15–20 cm]) deep
Water-plant or garden soil
Pebbles

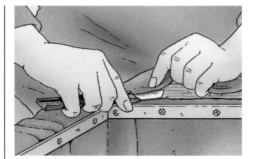

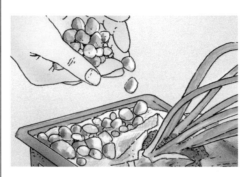

Leakproofing Wooden Troughs

Trace the interior dimensions of the
trough onto the lining and allow 2 in.
(5 cm) on all sides when cutting. Starting at a point in the center of a side of
the trough and working to the ends,
tack the lining to the top edge of the
trough, folding it in the corners. After
planting and filling with water, fasten
with a screwed-on aluminum strip and
cut off the lining that sticks up over it.

Basket Planting

Plants like water lilies are best placed
in baskets when they are planted; line
wide-meshed baskets ahead of time
with newspaper or jute.

Placing Plants

The top layer of the basket is weighted
with gravel to keep soil particles from
floating off. When setting the plants,
keep in mind their differing water-
depth requirements. Create the various different plant levels by means of
roof tiles or overturned flower pots.
Nonproliferating plants that need
water depths of 12–16 in. (30–40 cm)
can also be planted directly in the soil
of the container. It's best to use special water plants, as it is also for the
basket planting.

Before installing larger troughs, check the weight-bearing capacity of the deck. Stone and cement containers are only suitable for patios.

Putting in the Water

First cover the bottom of the container with gravel and larger pebbles. Let the water flow in indirectly and under weak pressure by using a pail so that neither pebbles nor soil are disturbed. The water should be warmed by the sun. Rainwater is recommended, especially in the case of plants sensitive to lime.

Plant and Maintenance Tips

The finished planted water garden has sweet flag (*Acorus calamus*; left); pickerel weed (*Pontederia cordata*; blue flowers), and pink water lily; in the substrate itself are planted a dwarf cattail (*Typha minima*) and an old world arrowhead (*Sagittaria sagittifolia*).

The best time for planting a water garden is between the beginning of May and the end of June. One of the trickiest jobs is the proper cutting and installation of the liner with as few folds as possible. If you have no desire to do that, you need to thoroughly study the other possible solutions: More and more often, there are ready-made products available, for instance tub inserts for rectangular and hexagonal troughs or special pond troughs with prepared liners and all the accessories installed.

A strong algae buildup initially, which also often occurs in hot summers, is no cause for alarm and, as a rule, it soon subsides again; always scoop the algae out. Other important maintenance jobs include: reining in rampant plants, regularly removing dead plant matter, and in summer, when there is rapid evaporation, refilling with a weak stream of water. Remove delicate plants from the pond in the fall and winter them over indoors in a bright, cool spot.

EXPERT TIP
Fertilize occasionally with special water-plant fertilizer.

CROSS-REFERENCE
Miniature Water Garden Focal Point pages 128–129

Safety and Legal Questions

	Critical Issues	Precautionary Measures
	**Balcony Use in Apartment Houses** The most important points of conflict and use restriction: possible damage to the rental premises, unusual design or even destruction of the "total architectonic-aesthetic impression."	Carefully clarify the structural alterations such as the addition of trellises with the landlord, especially unusual designs, such as natural plantings.
	**Weight-Bearing Capacity of the Balcony or Deck** Not only heavy containers (tropical plants, large ornamental shrubs, miniponds) but also floor coverings and massive furniture can stress the bearing capacity of floors and supporting walls.	Do not "push" the highest limit of 550 lb (250 kg) per 3 ft² (1 m²). In doubtful situations, have the structure and weight capacity checked by a civil engineer.
	**Damage by Climbing Plants** Vines with adhesive disks, like ivy, can injure the wall surface if the covering is already cracked; vigorous vines, for example, silver lace vine, can stop up drainpipes or crush them.	Train vines with adhesive disks on trellises attached to the wall; keep very vigorous varieties under control with clipping.
	**Attaching Flower Boxes** At the very latest, a storm wreaks vengeance for any negligence in fastening flower boxes on balconies or decks. Falling boxes or pots are dangerous to anyone underneath!	On higher floors, at least, carefully fasten boxes only on insides of railings and ledges; periodically check the brackets!

Make sure that you are in compliance with not only lease requirements but also all local zoning laws and weight-bearing capacities of your deck or terrace.

Critical Issues	Precautionary Measures

Water Damage
Constant water runoff leads to damage to the wall surfaces and can cause trouble with neighbors and passers-by.

Besides watering with care, saucers and outer pots, or larger containers used as outer pots (without drainage holes), head off problems later.

Plant Sprays
Plant sprays, even those with plant bases, often contain toxic ingredients that can injure humans and the environment. Those toxic to bees are automatically out of the question for flowering plants.

Use poisonous preparations only if it is absolutely unavoidable and follow the directions for use exactly. All plant sprays should be kept out of reach of children!

Danger from Plants
Some beautiful and popular plants are very poisonous; others can cause skin irritations. The danger of wounds is a threat with thorny plants, in particular.

Keep poisonous plants away from children. Wash hands after handling them. Wear gloves when working with irritating or well-armed plants; renew tetanus shots regularly.

Heavy Plant Containers
Heavy hothouse plants, potted shrubs, or miniponds have considerable weight, and unfortunately they do have to be moved now and again— with "do-it-yourself" moving there is high risk of back injury or accident.

Always have two people to move heavy pots and use aids such as wheelbarrows, plant trolleys, carrying straps, or pots with hand grips.

Maintenance

The famous "green thumb" is the combination of being well-informed, experience, enjoyment of plants—and a little instinct.

Plants are living things, and like all living things, they are not always predictable and are sometimes contrary. So, for example, you may have followed all the instructions and recommendations and, nevertheless, the new hothouse plants are not thriving as they should. And on the other hand, others that are in a spot that's too shady and are hardly fertilized are flowering nonstop.

Failure or Experience?
Obviously, the varied interplay among plants, weather, and the different growth factors cannot be controlled 100% in the minuscule "biome" of the deck planter. Occasional disappointments occur, even when "everything is done right." The optimist chalks this up to experience. And in fact, it does take some time, trial, and frequent working with plants to master the techniques.

Sometimes the disappointment may result from the "too good" care in the nursery from which the plants originate. In extreme cases, you can even get a plant that has been too carefully coddled until it is sold and doesn't survive the first few days on the deck. But even healthy, quality plant stock is raised under optimal culture conditions that you are not able to provide later. Sometimes plants simply need a certain period of acclimation until they are comfortable with the realities of life on balconies or decks and patios.

Basic Care: Watering and Fertilizing
That plants need water to live becomes obvious quickly and drastically when they are left unwatered for a few days in summer. Nutritional deficiencies manifest themselves rather more slowly through weaker growth, sparse bloom, or yellow leaves. Even so, regular fertilization is recommended for most plants, though in doubtful cases it's better to use less rather than more. In addition, proper watering and fertilizing prevent many diseases.

A few specific, regular procedures will ensure lasting pleasure in your green deck-dwellers.

Water, the Elixir of Life

Most deck plants can be watered with ordinary tap water or water from your hose outlet. However, if you live in an area with especially hard water, you may have problems with lime-sensitive plants like rhododendrons, citrus plants, and camellias. Hard water contains higher lime levels that can cause those plants to develop yellow leaves, stunted growth, and bud and flower drop.

You can ascertain the degree of hardness of your water by contacting your local water company. If your water is deemed even moderately hard, use a water-softening agent dissolved in a watering can before watering lime-sensitive plants. Rainwater, if you have a way to collect it, is excellent for watering these and all other plants.

Another solution for hard water areas is to use an acidic fertilizer when feeding plants.

With most plants, a good practice is to fill watering cans after each use and let them stand. This helps lower chlorine levels in the water as well as warming the water. Cold water directly out of the tap can be a shock for plants, especially younger ones.

Watering Tips

▶ As a rule, watering is done without the spray head so that you can get water to the roots directly. The plants themselves are scarcely dampened.

▶ Never water plants in the blazing sun (high evaporation, burning glass effect of water droplets on the leaves). Mornings and evenings are the best times.

▶ Don't water too late in the evening and make sure water gets between the leaves; when plants encounter cooler night temperatures with their leaves damp, some fungus diseases spread very easily.

▶ With plants that are placed high or are hanging, handy watering cans (available in 5- or 2.5-quart [L] versions) facilitate "handling" and precise watering without spilling. There are even watering cans with curving, extended spouts for hanging plants.

Oleander, the Exception

Unlike most plants, oleander does well when provided with a saucer that is always filled with water.

The Amount of Water Needed . . .

. . . depends very much on the plant and, of course, the season and the weather. Be guided by the pictographs with each of the plant portraits (page 57).

▶ "Much water" means that on hot summer days there must be watering up to twice daily. Along with certain species, plants in hanging baskets also have a very high water requirement.

▶ With "moderate" water requirements, watering is only done when the upper surface of the growing medium has dried out.

▶ "Little water" means that the growing medium in the root area should not dry out entirely (careful testing for moisture by feel).

Avoiding Overwatering

Constant wetness in the root region is lethal for most plants, except for those that are definitely swamp or water plants. Plants with bulbs and corms are particularly sensitive. The water not needed by the plant roots at the moment or that might be stored in the growing medium should be able to run off immediately.

▶ The most important preventive measures—besides providing water in the proper amounts—are the water drainage hole, drainage in the pot, and good potting soil.

Evaporation through leaves makes regular application of water to the roots essential.

► For plants that are very sensitive to soggy conditions in containers on the ground, a slightly raised position is recommended (for example, with "pot feet" from the garden center).

► To avoid sogginess, the saucers and outer pots, as well as water-storage containers without an outflow, should be emptied after heavy rainfall.

One of the few plants that tolerate "constant filling" of the plant saucer, in fact even loves it, is the oleander.

And When Vacation Rolls Around?
Containers with water reservoirs or watering mats sometimes make possible a long weekend without watering. But these solutions will not do for a vacation of several weeks in high summer. If friends or helpful neighbors aren't available as substitute waterers, the garden center offers different automatic watering systems for deck flower boxes and pots. It's best to inform yourself thoroughly

about what is suitable for your needs and purposes—the choices range from really simple equipment all the way to computer-controlled models.

Going through several trial runs before vacation to test whether the system functions flawlessly is an absolute must. One way or the other, it's a good idea to move the plants to a shady place before summer vacation.

Summer Maintenance Jobs

Information in Brief

Suitable Fertilizers

Liquid flower fertilizers, inorganic or organic, for mixing into the potting soil (organic or as coated granules)
Specialized fertilizers for certain plants, e.g., rhododendron/azalea fertilizer, conifer, and rose fertilizer, geranium fertilizer

Equipment, Tools

Several watering cans in different sizes (2$\frac{1}{2}$, 5, 10 qt [L])
Garden shears
Garden knife
Minihoe or old fork
Coconut matting for pot lining

Fertilizing
Regular fertilizing is begun 4–6 weeks after planting. It's easiest when the fertilizer is dissolved in water and applied with the watering can. The dosages given on the package should never be exceeded. Try not to wet the leaves or flowers when applying it. Also practical are slow-release fertilizers, which may or may not last for the entire growing season.

Removing Spent Flowers
Not only does this procedure, known as deadheading, benefit the overall visual effect, but usually the removal of wilted flowers also promotes the development of new flowers. Wilted blossoms can usually just be pinched off or picked; otherwise the shears must be used. With geraniums (pelargoniums) the flower stalk should be broken at the base, where it joins the stem. Wilted rhododendron flowers must be broken off very carefully, as the new growth buds are located just below them.

What you like for yourself on hot days is also good for plants: awnings or umbrellas protect from the searing midday sun.

Cutting Back After the First Flowering

With some plants, after the end of the main blooming period (early to mid summer), there is a more or less meager phase during which new flowers are formed. This second flowering can often be promoted by cutting back the shoots by a third or more immediately after the principal flowering. Candidates for this are, for instance, lobelias, sweet alyssum, argyranthemums and other daisy-type flowers (cut back only slightly), wax begonias, and large-flowered, upright to semi-cascading petunias.

Removing Spent Flowers

Leaves that have yellowed, dried out, or turned brown are pinched out regularly or carefully broken off at the base of the leaf stem. You should also immediately remove leaves, shoots, and flowers that show any symptoms of disease. This way, some ailments can be prevented before they get started.

Loosening the Soil in the Pot

When the surfaces of the potting medium in large pots and tubs get crusted and hard, they take up water poorly. At the same time, evaporation is increased through the development of fine pores. A cautious loosening (being careful not to injure roots) with an appropriately small tool, such as a sharpened stick or a fork, will help. Covering the upper surface of the pot with water-permeable coconut matting cut to size can also help to lessen evaporation and crusting.

EXPERT TIP
After storms and winds, cut off any bent stems right away.

Common Pests and Diseases

Pest/Disease	Description	Treatment and Tips
Aphids 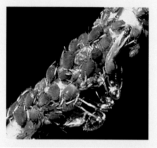	1–3 mm in size, usually green insects, in colonies, predominantly sitting on young shoots and undersides of leaves and sucking; leaves often rolled and sticky.	Often, dislodging the insects with a strong stream of water or brushing them off with a paper tissue is enough; nontoxic homemade spray: stinging nettle extract, soap solution.
Spider mites 	Tiny round animals, visible only with a magnifying glass, yellow-brown to reddish, sucking on the undersides of leaves; the leaves slowly yellow and wither; with a severe infestation, there is a covering of fine webs.	Occurs primarily in very dry-aired locations, also with too warm overwintering. Put affected plants in a cooler spot, keep them damp, rinse with lukewarm water, and mist often; spray if necessary.
Scale, mealybugs 	Scale: 1–3 mm long, roundish, yellow or brown, unmoving on stems and leaves, sucking; mealybugs: recognizable by cottony deposits on leaves, sticky leaves.	Often on hothouse plants wintered over too warm. Scratch off brown scale or deposits, treat with soap solution afterwards; with severe infestation, spray with preparations containing horticultural oils.
Whiteflies 	1–2 mm long white insects on the undersides of leaves, flying off when touched; sucking, leaves yellow and wither; frequent on fuchsias and lantanas.	Often on plants overwintered too warm; hang up yellow boards or yellow stickers covered with sticky material, spray with stinging nettle extract or insecticidal soap solution.

If applying a pesticide or fungicide appears unavoidable, you should choose preparations that are nontoxic to warm-blooded animals and that spare bees and other beneficials.

Pest/Disease	Description	Treatment and Tips
Snout weevils 	Beetle, 10 mm long, grayish black, active at dusk, eats edges of leaves; larvae whitish, with bright-brown head, lives in potting soil and eats plant roots.	Collect beetles after dark with a flashlight; larvae can be controlled biologically with parasitic nematodes (obtainable beginning in April from garden stores or by mail order).
Powdery mildew 	Harmful fungus, whitish, floury deposit develops on upper sides of leaves, also on flowers and buds. Common on begonias, roses, chrysanthemums, and zinnias.	Prevent by avoiding too much (nitrogen) fertilizing; don't plant too close together; when infection occurs, remove infected parts, treat several times with horsetail tea.
Downy mildew 	Harmful fungus, brown-gray, sticky deposits develop on leaves and other plant parts; often appears after rainy periods, frequently on begonias and strawberries.	Above all on injured, weakened plants; prevent with attention to optimal fertilization, not planting too densely; when it occurs, remove diseased plant parts, keep plants drier and with better air circulation.
Rust 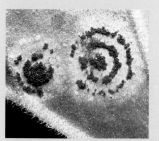	Harmful fungus, forms reddish pustules on the undersides of leaves, tops with light spots, leaves die off in time; often on geraniums (pelargoniums), fuchsias, carnations, and roses.	Remove diseased plant parts. The disease usually proceeds quickly; one has to decide: Would the use of a chemical fungicide be worth it or should the plant be removed entirely?

Supports and Trellises

Information in Brief

Appropriate Tying Materials

Garden twine
Natural or synthetic raffia
Coated wire

Stakes

Bamboo
Coated steel stakes
Fencing stakes for
high-growing deck tomatoes

Other Ways of Staking

Special metal supports for
tree forms with heavy crowns
Plant rings for potted plants
Perennial supports
Wire pyramids, posts, spirals,
or arches for placing in pots

Trellises

Wire or plastic lattices
Wooden wall trellises and
lattices
Free-standing deck trellises
(for boxes with climbing
plants)

Tying to Stakes

Supporting with a stake in the soil is particularly necessary for tree forms and container-grown fruit. Being a natural material, bamboo is very appropriate; such stakes are light, flexible, and yet very sturdy. Moreover, they hardly rot at all, even with prolonged contact with the soil. They are fastened with a figure-eight tie that is knotted to the stake. This tie must always be loose enough so that the stem or tree trunk will not be strangled as it thickens.

Support Rings

Some plants that grow tall tend to fall apart over time, for example, lilies, bamboos, or also some potted annuals like heliotrope. A remedy is provided by support rings, which are usually sold as perennial plant supports.

**Purchased supports and trellises are often
decorative elements as well. However, practicality
is still the most important criterion for choice.**

Trellises in Pots

The long climbers such as ivy, passionflower, or black-eyed Susan vine need not necessarily be trained up on "external" trellises. The garden center offers a rich selection of different types of trellises that can be stuck directly into the pots. Some, however, are only intended for indoor plants—so make sure they're made of weatherproof materials, such as plastic-coated wire, which must also be sturdy enough not to bend right over when the wind blows.

Supports and Trellises for Climbers

Wire or plastic lattices are practical and inexpensive, but the most attractive effects are achieved with expandable trellises and wall trellises of wood. For protection of the wall surface, the lattice should be at least 2 in. (5 cm) from the wall, and 4–5 in. (10–12 cm) would be even better. Therefore, first attach appropriately thick lathes or blocks as spacers. Not all plants necessarily require the construction of a trellis. Vines like scarlet runner beans and pipe vine will twine up on vertical wires, strings, and stakes.

Flower Boxes with Trellises

A practical and attractive way to grow vines is offered by flower boxes with integrated trellises. They are even available with large planters (for example, 39 × 20 × 20 in. [100 × 50 × 50 cm]), so that with enough space even perennial vines can be grown. As a rule, wooden boxes have been treated against rotting; for long-term planting, it's wise to do an additional treatment with a wood preservative that is nontoxic to plants. You must be sure to make water drainage holes in the bottom if they aren't there already.

EXPERT TIP
Sturdy supports are necessary for perennial climbing plants

CROSS-REFERENCES
Annual Vines pages 80–81
Woody Vines pages 96–97

Wintering Over

Information in Brief

Materials for Winter Protection

Leaves (healthy only)
Fir, pine branches
Styrofoam sheets
Coconut fiber pots, matting
Burlap
Agricultural fabric/floating row covers
Reed matting
Bubble-wrap (only for wrapping pots)

Regular Winter Checks

Plants outside:

Before night freeze, check the winter-protection materials
Water only when day temperatures are above freezing
Protect evergreens from late-winter sun

Plants inside:

Check for pests and disease
Remove fallen, yellowed, and dried leaves
Remove long, thin, yellow-leaved shoots in winter quarters
Water occasionally
Ventilate on days with above-freezing temperatures
Check temperature

Overwintering Outdoors

Ornamentals, fruits, and perennials that grow in the garden can be wintered over outdoors. All the eligible plants should be set in a protected place close to the house wall and clustered together. Prolonged freezing of the root ball is the greatest danger. In cases of doubt, the plant container should be protected all around: by placing it on a thick sheet of Styrofoam, wrapping with bubble-wrap, burlap, or with a commercially available "overpot" of coconut fiber. The top surface of the pot can also be covered with coconut matting or have leaves and evergreen branches laid over it. In subfreezing temperatures, the above-ground parts can be protected with wrappings of jute, burlap, agricultural fabric (no plastic sheets!), or with reed matting. Water occasionally on above-freezing days, especially the evergreen plants. Shade them on late-winter days.

All perennial plants, whether they spend the winter inside or outside, should receive no more fertilizer after the middle of August, at the latest.

Fall Grooming of Geraniums

Besides the hothouse plants, geraniums (pelargoniums) are top candidates for wintering over in the house. They are brought in before the first severe frost, about mid fall, at the very latest the end of October. They should be carefully cleaned, with the last flowers and wilted leaves removed. Never put the plants into winter quarters with wet roots; if necessary, let them dry first in a warmer place before you put them in a cool, bright spot.

Bringing in Hothouse Plants

Hothouse plants from the Mediterranean, tropical, or other warm regions must be wintered over indoors. Large plants can be transported more easily with hand trucks, plant dollies, or straps with handles, which can be purchased. Tie up the plants first, and disarm the dangerous points of agaves by sticking corks on them. A slight pruning can facilitate moving, but the chief pruning should be carried out in the spring.

Plants in Winter Quarters

It's a good idea to check hothouse and deck plants that are spending the winter indoors every week. You don't always have to have the ideal winter quarters. If the spot is a little too warm, provide some increased humidity, for instance by setting out water-filled saucers. Fuchsias, bougainvilleas, and some other pot plants will gradually lose their leaves if the location is too dark—no cause for concern, they are entering a resting phase. Starting in February or March, you can put the plants in a somewhat warmer—and thus possibly brighter—spot.

EXPERT TIP
A recommended utensil for winter quarters: a thermometer.

CROSS-REFERENCES
Ornamental Shrubs pages 88–97
Hothouse Plants pages 98–109

Pruning and Repotting

Information in Brief

Thinning and Pruning

Tools:
> Pruning shears
> Small pruning saw
> Wound paint

When:
> End of January to March

Time needed:
> 10–20 minutes per plant

Repotting

Tools/materials:
> New container ³/₄–3 in.
> (2–8 cm) wider than the
> old one
> Flower or specialized soil
> Slow-release fertilizer,
> possibly also sand and rock
> dust for mixing in
> Drainage material
> Sharp knife

When:
> From beginning of new growth
> to end of May

Time needed:
> 15–20 minutes per plant

Thinning

An annual thinning is recommended for almost all deciduous hothouse plants and potted woody plants. First, any branches that have died are taken right back to their bases, as are any shoots that are too close together or that grow toward the inside. Thin, very long shoots are shortened. If you are not entirely certain about whether to prune, first inspect the development of the shoot—better not to thin than to take off a flower-bearing branch (usually a one- or two-year-old shoot) by mistake.

Pruning

Pruning is recommended for plants that tend toward scraggly growth. In this case the entire shoot is shortened by cutting it back to just above a leaf bud that faces toward the outside. The severity of the pruning depends on the plant, but as a rule you should shorten by at least one-third. A clean cut is important—sharp pruning shears are an absolute must! Large pruning wounds, especially after a saw is used, should be painted with wound paint.

As usual, there are exceptions:
Agapanthus and old rosemaries are repotted
as seldom as possible.

Removing from the Old Pot

When plant roots have completely per-meated the potting soil, it is high time to repot. Often you will have to run a knife around the inside of the pot to free the roots from the pot wall, but sometimes it will be enough to loosen the soil in places with a sharpened stick. The new plant container should be wider than the old pot, 1–2 in. (2–4 cm) for young plants, 2–3 in. (6–8 cm) for larger, older ones.

Space-Saving Surgery

Vigorously growing species all too quickly come to the point when a larger container is no longer bearable, in the truest sense of the word. The solution: A wedge is cut out of the root ball with a sharp knife. This allows you to fill in with enough fresh soil mix without making a larger pot necessary. This works especially well with daturas and oleanders.

Repotting

The new pot (put clay pots in water for 1–2 days first) is filled with 1 in. (2–3 cm) of drainage material, for exam-ple pebbles or perlite. Then some soil is filled in and the plant is temporarily set in the pot to check for height. The top of the root ball should come to just 1 in. (2–3 cm) below the rim of the pot, the depth of the watering space later. The soil is evened as needed, the remaining space filled in with more soil and firmed. Finally the repotted plant is watered thoroughly and placed in a somewhat warmer spot.

EXPERT TIP
Cut away dead root tips before repotting.

CROSS-REFERENCES
Hothouse Plants pages 98–109
Ornamental Shrubs pages 88–97

Year-Round Maintenance

Month	Jobs, Maintenance
January/February 	Regularly inspect deck and hothouse plants that are being wintered over; check outdoor frost protection, water evergreens after periods of below-freezing temperatures; order seeds; start geraniums to be grown from seed, from Feburary other deck flowers too; prune geraniums, hothouse plants, and potted woody plants, repot if necessary (till end of May).
March 	Plant spring containers with purchased plants; start annuals, vegetables, and herbs from seed, prick out first seeds; place hothouse plants in warmer locations, inspect carefully for pests; prune the last hothouse plants and potted woody plants; clean plant containers, buy new as needed.
April 	Order plants, if necessary; start more annuals, vegetables, and herbs, prick out; pinch back young plants grown from seed; plant ornamentals and fruits in tubs; begin fertilizing hothouse plants, water more often; harden off plants outside on warm days.
May 	Buy deck flowers; still repot hothouse plants if necessary; after all danger of frost is past, put boxes and plants outside, insofar as weather permits; for particularly sensitive ones, wait till the end of May; cover when late frosts threaten.

**Optimal plant care can
become a passion. But don't neglect enjoyment by spending all your time watering!**

Month	Jobs, Maintenance
June 	Begin fertilizing deck flowers; water regularly and remove spent flowers; start seeds of biennials like English daisies and violas; clean out the spring displays if flowers are finished; plant water garden.
July/August 	Water, water, water! Fertilize regularly and remove spent flowers; before going on vacation, arrange for a substitute (friend, neighbor, automatic watering system), move plants to shady places; by mid August, stop fertilizing all candidates for wintering over.
September/October 	Start seeds for fall and winter planting; plant spring boxes and pots with spring bulbs; move sensitive plants inside before the first frost, then gradually—depending on frost-hardiness—all other hothouse plants; provide protection for plants wintering over outside and for water gardens; bring in miniponds that not frost-proof; clear out summer flower boxes, if flowers finished.
November/December 	Regularly inspect deck and hothouse plants that are being wintered over, water evergreens after periods of below-freezing temperatures; pore through catalogs and magazines, plan new plantings and designs.

Choosing Plants

Choosing Plants

Look for Appropriate Species

Almost every year, the already huge assortment of deck plants is expanded by still more new hybrids and newly introduced species. Necessarily, the following selections are limited to especially tried-and-true and popular plants that will offer you a wealth of design possibilities. In addition, in the chapter on design, you will find suggestions for plants with particular characteristics, such as fragrance or unusual foliage. Nurseries and garden centers cannot keep everything on hand: If you set your heart on a very particular plant, the only possible solution may be to get it from a mail-order nursery (see Buying Plants and Seeds, pages 14–15; you will find addresses of garden magazines in the appendix). The vast diversity of species and varieties sometimes makes for confusion (see also Species, Varieties, Hybrids on pages 150–151). Please bear in mind that varieties, specific forms of one and the same plant, can differ in not only color but also growth height, form, and flowering time, even their tolerance for shade, from the original.

Arrangement of the Portrait Section
The first three chapters are concerned with deck flowers, the majority of which can be combined in boxes but can also be decorative in pots, saucer planters, and hanging pots and baskets.

▶ Deck plant portraits are separated into spring, summer, and late-blooming flowers, in order to help you design a deck that is in bloom nearly year-round.

▶ The countless summer flowers imprint color from June well into October. They are divided according to light requirements, the most important criterion for choice.

▶ The ornamental shrubs that follow these sections expand the design possibilities, for instance with evergreens for winter plantings and perennial vines that are suitable for pot culture.

▶ Then follow portraits of hothouse plants, those natives of warmer countries that must be wintered over inside. They are classed according to sun or shade tolerance.

▶ Finally, the last chapter presents a few useful plants that are particularly suitable for deck and patio.

Along with vegetables and fruit, there are sections on annual and perennial herbs, which can also be grown very successfully in a small space.

Format of Plant Portraits
The individual plant portraits are in the following format:
▶ The common name in English is given. Since newly introduced

varieties, especially, are often sold under various names, the botanical name listed underneath eliminates any doubt about which plant is meant.
▶ The information about height always follows a short note about the growth habit to facilitate the selection and combination of different plants; with deck flowers there is additional information about the best planting distance under the heading "Planting."

These specifications are approximate; they can vary according to variety and growing conditions.
▶ The same goes for the information below it about flowering season (replaced by harvest time with food plants), which can vary according to the time of planting.
▶ The fifth line tells which plant category the particular genus or species belongs to.
▶ The pictographs used (see right) show at one glance a plant's most important light and watering requirements and any special features.
▶ Underneath that is a note about particular characteristics or virtues of the plant under discussion or about any special requirements.
▶ The hardiness zone gives the range of zones in which the plant can be reliably grown. Determine your growing zone from the map on page 157.

The Pictographs Used

 The plant wants it bright and sunny (south-, west-, east-facing deck)

 The plant thrives best in part shade (east-, west-, bright north-facing deck)

 The plant thrives well even in full shade (north-, dark east-, west-facing deck)

 The plant needs much water (in general, daily)

 The plant needs a moderate amount of water (about every 2–3 days)

 The plant needs very little water (do not let it dry out)

 The plant is effective in hanging pots and baskets

 The plant is poisonous or irritating to the skin

Bear in mind that even in nonpoisonous plants, the seeds may contain toxic elements!

Even a small deck can be decorated with a profusion of plants by taking advantage of several levels, with pots hanging and on the floor.

Notes on the plant descriptions and maintenance instructions:

Flowers: It is always the principal colors that are given, but very often there are infinitely various shadings—depending on the variety—among the main hues. Also, the flower forms can differ as a result of hybridizing. In entries on plants with decorative leaves and fruits, there are notes on the ornamental value instead.

Growing: Amplifying the chapter on raising plants (starting page 16), there are special notes in this section about growing from seed. Unless otherwise noted, the plants are dark-germinators.

Planting: Gives the time for planting or moving plant containers outside and, in the case of deck flowers, the best planting distances from other plants.

Care: Supplementing the information in the chapter on plant care, this section lists special plant requirements and chores. You will also find advice on overwintering perennial plants here.

Propagating: This offers special notes on propagation by cuttings.

Design: Under this heading are tips and suggestions for using or combining the particular plant for the best visual effects.

Spring Flowers

**Always a special event:
the first flowers after the dark of
winter. Some early bloomers last
into the beginning of summer.**

The deck season begins with snowdrops and crocuses, and soon after tulips, narcissi, pansies, English daisies, etc., provide the feeling of spring. Many spring flowers are especially lovely in shallow bulb pans or saucer planters, but they are also effective pots or in flower boxes and among dwarf evergreens.

Spring Glory with Bulbs and Corms

Bulbs or corms are often planted in their containers in September/ October. In regions with mild winters you can leave them outside, covered with pine branches. However, it is safer to winter them over in a bright spot in a frost-proof area. A warm situation is not an advantage, just the opposite: Bulbs or corms will only sprout if they are kept cool. The simpler alternative to fall planting is buying already-started plants in the spring. Especially with bulbs and corms, make sure that planting soil always remains slightly damp but is never completely soaking, because otherwise the vital organs

underground may rot. When used in plant containers, these bulbs and corms are not usually sturdy enough to regrow reliably or well the next year. However, if you have a garden, you can plant the bulbs there after they've finished blooming and the above-ground foliage has disappeared completely.

Pansies and Such

With their special life cycle—leaf formation in the year they are sown, flowers the following season—the biennials give us some of the most attractive spring flowers. In this case, too, there is either the possibility of starting the plants yourself and wintering them over (with protection) or putting in plants bought in the spring. Besides the short-lived biennials, primulas and violas are perennials, plants that die down and sprout again in the spring. But with these, too, continuing culture is only worthwhile in the garden, as a rule, except for certain violet varieties.

*Bulbs make their grand entrance in
March and provide the first splashy
show of flowers of the year.*

Bulbs and Corms

Crocus
Crocus species
Height: 4–6 in. (10–15 cm), upright
Blooms: February–April, depending on species
Bulb

▶ **colorful spring thrill**

Flowers: Yellow, white, pink, violet, also multicolored; cup- or goblet-shaped. **Planting:** Plant corms 2½–3 in. (6–8 cm) deep, 2–4 in. (5–10 cm) apart in September/October. **Care:** Winter over outside, protected with branches; better still, keep above freezing in the dark, not allowing soil to dry out; when sprouting begins, place in the light, water moderately, fertilize once after flowering begins. **Design:** Very beautiful in combinations of different-colored crocus species and varieties and as flowering accents in permanent plantings. **Zone:** 4–9 (depending upon species).

Snowdrop
Galanthus nivalis
Height: 4–6 in. (10–15 cm); upright, dainty
Blooms: February–March
Bulb

▶ **the first messengers of spring**

Flowers: Little white bells, inner petals edged with green. **Planting:** Plant bulbs 4 in. (10 cm) deep, 1½ in. (4 cm) apart in September. **Care:** Protect over winter outside with branches; better still, keep inside in a cool, dark spot, never letting soil dry out; move into bright light to part-shade when new growth shows, water moderately, fertilize once after flowers appear. **Design:** In bulb pans and boxes alone or with crocuses; underplanting of shrubs in tubs, between perennials. **Zone:** 3–8.

Hyacinth
Hyacinthus orientalis
Height: 8–12 in. (20–30 cm); upright
Blooms: April–May
Bulb

▶ **intense, sweet fragrance**

Flowers: All colors, in large, closely packed racemes. **Planting:** In spring, place forced bulbs 6–8 in. (15–20 cm) deep, 4–6 in. (10–15 cm) apart. Planting in fall is possible but risky. **Care:** Keep in a cool, dark place, above freezing, never letting soil dry out; then move to bright light, water moderately, fertilize once after flowering begins; cut off stems when flowers are finished. **Design:** Since the area around the stalks looks a little bare, additional plantings of shorter spring flowers with basal leaves are recommended. **Zone:** 4–8.

EXPERT TIP
Attractive species are **Crocus chrysanthus** *and* **Crocus vernus.**

GOOD PARTNERS
Pansies, primulas, English daisies

Spring-flowering bulbs and corms create the most beautiful effects when they are planted together in small groups.

Grape Hyacinth
Muscari species
Height: 6–10 in. (15–25 cm); upright, dainty
Blooms: March–May
Bulb

▶ **infinitely combinable**

Flowers: Racemes of little blue bell flowers; *M. botryoides* 'Alba' has white flowers. **Planting:** Plant bulbs 2–3 in. (5–8 cm) deep, 1½–3 in. (4–8 cm) apart in September. **Care:** Keep in a dark place, cool but above-freezing, over winter, never allowing soil to dry out; when first growth shows, move to part shade, water moderately, fertilize once after flowering begins. **Design:** Decorative spots of spring color under shrubs and in perennial plantings (plant there in fall, protect well with branches over winter). **Zone:** 3–9.

Narcissus
Narcissus species
Height: 6–24 in. (15–60 cm); upright
Blooms: March–April, depending on variety
Bulb

▶ **sometimes fragrant**

Flowers: Yellow, yellow-orange, white, also bicolors; trumpet- or flat-cupped. **Planting:** Plant bulbs 2–4 in. (5–10 cm) deep, 2½–4 in. (6–10 cm) apart in September. **Care:** Keep above freezing in a cool, dark place over winter, never allowing soil to dry out; when growth begins, move to a bright to semishady spot, water moderately, fertilize once after flowering begins. **Design:** In combinations with other species, be careful about the different blooming times of narcissus varieties; reliable variety: 'Ceylon': yellow and gold, 14 in. (35 cm) tall, midseason blooming. **Zone:** 3–9.

Tulip
Tulipa species
Height: 4–24 in. (10–60 cm] depending on species and culture; upright
Blooms: depending on variety, March–May
Bulb

▶ **use only low-growing varieties**

Flowers: All colors except blue, also multicolored, bell- to goblet-shaped. **Planting:** Plant bulbs 4 in. (10 cm) deep in September, 2 in. (5 cm) apart. **Care:** Keep above freezing in a cool, dark place over winter, never allowing soil to dry out; move to bright light to part-shade when growth begins, water moderately, fertilize once after flowering begins; cut stems of spent flowers back halfway. **Design:** Place in combinations with other spring bloomers in small groups of 4–5 plants. **Zone:** 3–8.

GOOD PARTNERS
Goes with all spring flowers

GOOD PARTNERS
English daisies, grape hyacinths, tulips

EXPERT TIP
Small wild tulips (botanical tulips) are particularly charming.

Biennials and Perennials

English Daisy
Bellis perennis
Height: 4–6 in. (10–15 cm); compact, rosette-leaved
Blooms: March–June
Biennial

▶ **attractive shape and color**

Flowers: White, pink, red; single or doubled to pom-pom-shape. **Growing:** From seed in June/July, light-germinator; place in part shade, prick out to individual pots. **Planting:** In fall (winter protection, don't allow soil to dry out) or spring, 4–6 in. (10–15 cm) apart. **Care:** Water moderately, on warm days copiously, fertilize every 2 weeks, remove spent flowers regularly. **Design:** Goes particularly well with all blue spring flowers like grape hyacinths, forget-me-nots, and hyacinths. **Zone:** 3–8.

Wallflower
Cheiranthus cheiri
Height: 12–18 in. (30–45 cm); upright
Blooms: April–June
Grown as biennial

▶ **honeylike scent**

Flowers: Yellow, orange, reddish brown; 3/4–1 in. (2–3 cm) across, in racemes, single or double. **Growing:** From seed from May to July, prick out into individual pots. **Planting:** In fall (winter protection) or spring, 6–8 in. (15–20 cm) apart. **Care:** Keep slightly damp all the time, fertilize every 2 weeks, remove spent flowers regularly. **Design:** The recommended varieties (for example, 'Fire King', 'Blood Red') are mostly bright color mixtures; blue forget-me-nots go best with them. **Zone:** 3–8.

Forget-me-not
Myosotis sylvatica
Height: 6–14 in. (15–35 cm); bushy
Blooms: April–June
Perennial grown as biennial

▶ **blues of every shade**

Flowers: Blue, pink, white; countless tiny little individual flowers. **Growing:** Seed in July; place in part shade, prick out into individual pots. **Planting:** In fall (winter protection) or spring, 6 in. (15 cm) apart. **Care:** Water copiously on warm days, fertilizer not necessary. **Design:** Depending on the variety, light- to lavender-blue makes a pretty contrast with white, yellow, and red spring flowers; loosens up the stiff forms of flowering bulbs. **Zone:** 4–8.

GOOD PARTNERS
Forget-me-nots, pansies

GOOD PARTNERS
Tulips, narcissi, wallflowers, pansies

These varieties are attractive companions for flowering bulbs and are excellent for filling spaces until the flush of summer flowers.

English Primrose
Primula vulgaris hybrids
Height: 6 in. (15 cm); cushionlike
Blooms: March–May
Perennial grown as annual

▶ **delicately fragrant flowers**

Flowers: All colors including violet, also multicolors; plate-shaped in clusters. **Growing:** Difficult; buy plants, starting in February. **Planting:** In spring, 6–8 in. (15–20 cm) apart. **Care:** Consistently keep slightly damp, fertilizer not necessary. **Design:** Saucer planters with different-colored varieties look very attractive; go well with color-coordinated tulips, narcissi, and hyacinths. **Zone:** 3–8.

Viola
Viola cornuta hybrids
Height: 4–6 in. (10–15 cm); compact
Blooms: April–September
Perennial, sometimes only biennial

▶ **also called the horned violet**

Flowers: All colors, also multicolored; small, very dainty. **Growing:** When sown in July, bright, cool overwintering is required; better to buy plants already raised. **Planting:** In March/April, 4–8 in. (10–20 cm) apart. **Care:** Water copiously on warm days, fertilize once, at most, cut off stems of flowers that have finished blooming; perennial varieties can be continued in cultivation when flowering is finished. **Design:** Attractive in shallow saucer planters or as partners with tulips, especially the blue-violet varieties like 'Jersey Gem'. **Zone:** 5–8.

Pansy
Viola Wittrockiana hybrids
Height: 6–10 in. (15–25 cm); compact
Blooms: March–June (also in fall)
Annual/Tender perennial

▶ **gigantic range of colors**

Flowers: All colors, also multicolored; small- or large-flowered, up to 4 in. (10 cm). **Growing:** From seed in June/July; place in part shade, prick out into individual pots. **Planting:** In fall (winter protection, do not let soil dry out) or spring, 4–6 in. (10–15 cm) apart. **Care:** Water moderately, copiously on warm days, fertilize every 2 weeks; remove spent flowers. **Design:** The commonly available color mixtures look very beautiful in saucer planters.

EXPERT TIP
Attractive relative: the yellow cowslip (Primula veris)

EXPERT TIP
Also sold as minipansies (Viola hybrida)

GOOD PARTNERS
Tulips, hyacinths, narcissi

Summer Flowers

**With early summer, the entire palette
of colors and shapes becomes available.
Supported by certain perennials,
the summer annuals steal the show.**

Although there are many attractive "summer flowers" that are perennial, blooming year after year, the term is used here to mean annuals, plants that die back after flowering and do not put out new growth again. And so during their short life-span they provide a simply extravagant abundance of blossoms, often straight into fall.

Not Only Sun-Worshipers

You can easily imagine that plants that put forth so much new growth and flowers need a lot of energy—and thus a great deal of sun, more or less. The classification of the following portraits gives you a clue as to which plants will be most likely to thrive in the light conditions on your deck. But you may certainly look beyond your own deck and dare to experiment. Some of the same plants will thrive with less good light, it's just that then the flowers may not be so luxuriant. And the breeders are always striving to create shade-tolerant varieties. On the other hand, increasingly, sun-tolerant hybrids of fuchsia, begonias, and impatiens, all decorative plants for (part) shade originally, are being developed.

Diversity of Forms

Please consider the arrangement of the following text according to large and small plants a guideline only. Thus *large* embraces not only the height of growth but also the space requirement or the dominant appearance in a mixed planting. Even in such species, more and more often there are dwarf and trailing forms available. Thus you will find suitable plants for hanging pots and baskets not only in the section entitled "Hanging Pots and Trailing Plants." The outstanding beauties for such use are presented there, of course, but for the other species also, the appropriate pictograph (see page 57) will indicate when hanging varieties are available. Don't forget the annual vines, which in a very short time provide an attractive leafy privacy screen and display of summer flowers.

*Early summer sees the start of the
enormous displays of the annuals, which
often last right into the fall.*

Sun-Worshiping Flowers

Asteriscus

Asteriscus maritimus
Height: 10–12 in. (25–30 cm); broad; trailing
Blooms: April/May–October
Perennial

▶ **weather-fast suns of flowers**

Flowers: Golden-yellow, like little sunflowers. **Growing:** As tip cuttings without flower buds, cut back in August, winter over cool and bright. **Planting:** From middle of May, 8–10 in. (20–25 cm). **Care:** Keep uniformly damp, fertilize weekly; regularly cut off spent flowers; can be wintered over in a bright spot at about 50° F (10° C). **Design:** Beautiful as slightly trailing "corner plant" in boxes, also can be used as a hanging plant. Caution: vigorous growth habit; can overwhelm more weakly growing plants! **Zone:** 7–10, or can be grown as an annual in colder zones.

Tickseed

Coreopsis verticillata
Height: up to 24 in. (60 cm)
Blooms: May–September
Perennial cultivated as annual

▶ **flowers very lush and long**

Flowers: Bright yellow, star-shaped. **Growing:** Easiest to buy plants or start seed in early spring. Will often self-sow once established. **Planting:** Early spring or fall, 15–18 in. (35–45 cm) apart. **Care:** Tolerates heat and dry soil, full sun; regularly snip off spent flowers; divide as needed in the spring or fall. In very hot areas, benefits from some afternoon shade. **Design:** Beautiful in boxes; very attractive with blue cascading petunias or hanging verbenas. **Zone:** 4–9.

Cape Marigold

Dimorphotheca sinuata, D. pluvialis
Height: 12–15 in. (30–38 cm); upright, bushy
Blooms: May–September
Annual

▶ **a beauty for hot, dry areas**

Flowers: Yellow, orange, white, rose; daisylike, up to 3 in. (8 cm) Ø; open only in sun. **Growing:** from seed in March; also sowing directly in flower boxes possible after beginning of May. **Planting:** From mid May, 10–12 in. (25–30 cm) apart. **Care:** Water sparingly, fertilize every 2 weeks; after end of June cut away spent flowers; if possible, protect from rain. **Design:** Rainproof partners balance out "bad-weather losses" but should also be able to do with little water, for instance, lavender, sweet alyssum, campanulas.

EXPERT TIP
A tried-and-true deck variety is 'Gold Coin'.

EXPERT TIP
Good choices for containers are Coreopsis 'Moonbeam' and 'Zagreb'.

EXPERT TIP
The related Osteospermum *is native to South Africa.*

These plants cope effortlessly with the brilliant midday sun on a south-facing deck and thrive anyplace where it is constantly sunny and warm.

Livingstone Daisy
Dorotheanthus bellidiformis
Height: 2–6 in. (5–15 cm); low, spreading
Blooms: July–September
Annual

▶ **usually available in color mixture**

Flowers: White, yellow, orange, rose, red, violet; daisylike, up to 2 in. (5 cm) Ø; opens only in sun. **Growing:** From seed in March/April, sow individually in pots; also direct sowing in boxes at the beginning of May possible. **Planting:** From mid May, 8 in. (20 cm) apart. **Care:** Keep almost dry, do not fertilize. **Design:** Go well with other sun-worshiping flowers like portulaca; decorative in shallow saucer planters that are arranged with Mediterranean hothouse plants.

Gazania
Gazania hybrids
Height: 8–12 in. (20–30 cm); flat leaf rosettes
Blooms: June–October
Perennial usually raised as annual

▶ **glowing composite flowers**

Flowers: Yellow, yellow-orange, red, rose, white, often with ringed marking, up to 4 in. (10 cm) Ø; open only in the sun. **Growing:** From seed indoors from February to April, barely cover seeds. **Planting:** From mid May (after last frost), 12 in. (30 cm) apart. **Care:** Tolerates dry soil; allow soil to dry between watering; fertilize weekly; regularly cut off spent flowers; if possible, arrange protection from rain. **Design:** Low but striking companion for taller species, which should also not have a very great need for water.

Portulaca, Moss Rose
Portulaca grandiflora
Height: 6–8 in. (15–20 cm); ground-hugging, spreading
Blooms: June–September
Annual

▶ **enchanting mixtures of colors**

Flowers: Yellow, orange, red, pink, rose, white, 1 to 3 in. (8 cm) Ø; opens only in sunshine. **Growing:** From seed from March to May; sowing directly in flower boxes is also possible after beginning of May. **Planting:** From mid May, 6 in. (15 cm) apart. **Care:** Water scantily, fertilize every 4–6 weeks; protect from rain if possible. **Design:** Only available in mixtures with brilliant and some light pastel colors, portulaca is effective without other companions despite its low growth habit; 'Sundial Hybrid Mix' is suitable for hanging pots.

GOOD PARTNERS
Blue marguerite, heliorope, scarlet sage

GOOD PARTNERS
Cape marigolds, Livingstone daisies, lunaria

Sun-Loving Large Flowers

Dahlia
Dahlia hybrids
Height: 12–24 in. (30–60 cm); upright, bushy
Blooms: July–October
Tuber/Tender perennial

▶ **use only dwarf forms**

Flowers: White, yellow, rose, red; varieties are often mixed colors; single or double. **Growing:** From seed in February/March, sow 2–3 seeds per pot. **Planting:** From mid May, 12 in. (30 cm) apart. **Care:** High water requirement, fertilize weekly; regularly remove spent flowers; provide wind protection if possible. **Design:** Best effect in plant containers when used alone or combined with trailing ornamental-leaved plants such as Swedish ivy. **Zone:** 9–11.

Blue Marguerite, Blue Daisy
Felicia amelloides
Height: 8–20 in. (20–50 cm); upright, bushy
Blooms: May–October
Annual

▶ **tireless, long-flowering plant**

Flowers: Blue with yellow centers; marguerite-like, with a good 1 in. (3 cm) Ø. **Growing:** From cuttings that are taken in August/September; winter over in a cool, bright spot, pinch back young plants. **Planting:** From mid May, 8–10 in. (20–25 cm) apart. **Care:** Do not allow to dry out, fertilize every 2 weeks; cut off spent flower branches; may be wintered over (bright, about 54° F [12° C]) **Design:** Can be used in mixed boxes but also alone as handsome container plants.

Common Sunflower
Helianthus annuus
Height: 16–24 in. (40–60 cm); upright (dwarf varieties)
Blooms: July–October
Annual

▶ **choose special pot or dwarf varieties**

Flowers: Yellow, orange, red-brown, with dark center; single or double (e.g., the variety 'Teddy Bear'). **Growing:** From seed in April, sow seeds in individual pots. **Planting:** From mid May, 8–10 in. (20–25 cm) apart. **Care:** High water requirement, fertilize weekly; put in as wind-sheltered a spot as possible; grows in almost any soil. **Design:** Attractive in large pots, especially underplanted with lobelias; well-branched varieties like 'Elf' (16 in. [40 cm] tall) bloom especially well.

EXPERT TIP
Recommended also are the very floriferous mignon dahlias.

GOOD PARTNERS
Calceolaria, nemesia, petunias

These plants require mainly unobtrusive partners. They are also extremely effective on their own and sometimes are easy on the nose, as well.

Heliotrope

Heliotropium arborescens

Height: 12–24 in. (30–60 cm); upright, bushy

Blooms: May–September

Tender perennial, raised as an annual

▶ **pleasantly fragrant**

Flowers: Blue, purple; large clusters of numerous tiny florets. **Growing:** From seed in February/March, light-germinator; pinch back young plants; from cuttings in fall. **Planting:** From mid May, 10 in. (25 cm) apart. **Care:** Do not let dry out, fertilize weekly; regularly remove spent flowers; arrange for rain protection. **Design:** Compact varieties like 'Dwarf Marine' are useful for mixed boxes; also available in tree form (winter over bright at 54°–59° F [12°–15° C]).

Tobacco Plant, Flowering Tobacco

Nicotiana × alata

Height: 12–36 in. (30–90 cm); upright, bushy

Blooms: July–September

▶ **delicate, sweet evening fragrance**

Flowers: White, yellow, rose, red; tubes with starlike head. **Growing:** From seed in February/March, light-germinator; best to prick out two times. **Planting:** From mid May, 10–12 in. (25–30 cm) apart. **Care:** High water requirement, fertilize weekly; cut off spent flower panicles. **Design:** Mixed colors work well without any companions, sometimes in large saucer planters; in mixed boxes, for instance, with lobelias or verbenas, domineering plants.

Butterfly Flower

Schizanthus × wisetonensis hybrids

Height: 12–24 in. (30–60 cm); upright, bushy

Blooms: July–September

Annual

▶ **charming, exotic flowers**

Flowers: Rose, red, pink, purple, often flecked or veined; slit petals look like fringe. **Growing:** From seed in March/April. **Planting:** From mid May, 12 in. (30 cm) apart. **Care:** Always keep slightly damp, fertilize weekly; regularly remove spent flowers; will bloom again when cut back after the first flowering (about beginning of August). **Design:** Hardly needs a companion, attractive in mixtures like 'Hit Parade' or 'Boquet'. Best for areas with cool summers.

GOOD PARTNERS
Marigolds, geraniums (pelargoniums), sweet alyssum

EXPERT TIP
One reliable variety is the mixed-color 'Nicki' series.

Sun-Loving Medium-Sized Flowers

Annuals for Sunny Locations

Name	Height Growth Habit	Flower Color When Blooms
Cockscomb, Celosia (*Celosia argentea*)	8–12 in. (20–30 cm) bushy	rose, red, yellow July–September
Diascia (*Diascia* species)	8–16 in. (20–40 cm) semitrailing	rose, violet June–October
Pinks (*Dianthus chinensis*)	8–12 in. (20–30 cm) bushy	rose, red, white June–September
Dahlberg daisy (*Dyssodia tenuiloba*)	4–6 in. (10–15 cm) trailing	yellow June–October
California poppy (*Eschscholzia californica*)	12–24 in. (30–60 cm) bushy	yellow, orange, white June–October
Globe amaranth (*Gomphrena globosa*)	12–24 in. (30–60 cm) bushy	white, rose, red, violet July–October
Strawflower, Everlasting (*Helichrysum bracteatum*)	10–24 in. (25–60 cm) bushy	white, yellow, rose, red, violet July–October
Nemesia (*Nemesia* hybrids)	12–18 in. (30–45 cm) semitrailing	all colors May–September
Annual phlox (*Phlox drummondii*)	6–20 in. (15–50 cm) bushy	white, yellow, rose, violet June–September
Mealy-cup sage (*Salvia farinacea*)	12–18 in. (30–45 cm) upright	blue, violet, white June–October
Scarlet sage (*Salvia splendens*)	8–20 in. (20–50 cm) bushy	red, rose May–September
Nasturtium (*Tropaeolum* hybrids)	10–20 in. (25–50 cm) bushy/ trailing	yellow, orange, red June–October
Zinnia (*Zinnia* species)	6–36 in. (15–90 cm) bushy	all colors except blue June–September

China Aster
Callistephus chinensis
Height: 6–36 in. (15–90 cm); bushy, wide
Blooms: July–October
Annual

▶ **often sold in mixture of colors**

Flowers: White, rose, red, purple, blue, often with striking yellow centers; usually double, semispherical to pom-pomlike. **Growing:** From seed in March/April. **Planting:** From mid May, 8–10 in. (20–25 cm) apart. **Care:** Water plentifully in hot spells, fertilize weekly; regularly remove spent flowers. **Design:** In combination with cushion asters, adorn the deck until fall.

Felecia
Coleostephus, Hymenostemma
Height: 8–16 in. (20–40 cm); bushy
Blooms: May–September/October
Annual

▶ **single varieties with meadow appeal**

Flowers: Yellow (*Coleostephus multicaulis*), white (*Hymenostemma paludosum*); single or double. **Growing:** From seed in March, cover very thinly. **Planting:** From mid May, 8–12 in. (20–30 cm) apart. **Care:** Keep evenly damp, fertilize weekly; regularly cut off spent flowers; cut back *H. paludosum* after first flowering. **Design:** Goes with all sun-loving flowers that don't grow too vigorously; very similar to low-growing argyranthemum (see page 102).

GOOD PARTNERS
Felecia, sweet alyssum, lobelia

EXPERT TIP
Often still sold under the former name Chrysanthemum

Combinations of yellow, orange, and warm red have a truly sunny effect; white, rose, and blue are visually cool.

Sanvitalia

Sanvitalia procumbens
Height: 3–6 in. (8–15 cm); branching, trailing
Blooms: June–October
Annual

▶ **sometimes called creeping zinnia**

Flowers: Yellow with black centers; star-shaped, buttonlike, numerous. **Growing:** From seed in March. **Planting:** From mid May, 4–6 in. (10–15 cm) apart. **Care:** Always keep slightly damp, fertilize with weakened dose every 2 weeks; regularly cut off spent flowers; place where protected from rain. **Design:** Attractive as trailing front plants along the edges of boxes; also suitable as hanging plants.

Marigold

Tagetes species and hybrids
Height: 8–36 in. (20–90 cm); upright, bushy
Blooms: May/July–October
Annual

▶ **choose low-growing varieties**

Flowers: Yellow, orange, red, red-brown, also bicolors; single (*T. tenuifolia*) or double, all the way to pom-pomlike (*T. patula* and *T. erecta* hybrids). **Growing:** From seed from March to May. **Planting:** From mid May, 6–10 in. (15–25 cm) apart. **Care:** Keep evenly damp, fertilize monthly, regularly remove spent flowers. **Design:** Often sold in mixed colors, with which warm, glowing red or blue partners go especially well.

Verbena, Vervain

Verbena hybrids
Height: 12–18 in. (30–45 cm); upright/trailing
Blooms: June–October
Annual

▶ **delightful hanging forms**

Flowers: Blue, purple, white, red, rose; umbel-like umbrellas with little individual flowers. **Growing:** Difficult, better to buy young plants. **Planting:** From mid May, 8 in. (20 cm) apart. **Care:** High water requirement, fertilize every 3 weeks; regularly remove spent flowers. **Design:** Upright to creeping forms with varied uses; hanging verbenas ('Homestead Purple' varieties) very attractive as front plantings and in hanging pots.

GOOD PARTNERS
Geraniums (pelargoniums), ageratums, heliotrope

EXPERT TIP
The fragrant T. tenuifolia *is also called "signet marigold."*

EXPERT TIP
Caution: The hanging varieties, in particular, are robust growers!

Medium-Sized Flowers Tolerating Shade

Wax Begonia
Begonia semperflorens hybrids
Height: 6–16 in. (15–40 cm); upright, compact
Blooms: May–October
Perennial raised as annual

▶ **does best in part shade**

Flowers: White, rose, red, also bicolored; up to 2 in. (5 cm) Ø, single or double. **Growing:** Difficult, better to buy young plants. **Planting:** From mid May, 6–10 in. (15–25 cm) apart. **Care:** Always keep well watered but under no circumstances soggy; fertilize lightly every 3 weeks; regularly remove spent flowers; cut back after first flowering. **Design:** In some varieties, dark or reddish-brown foliage provides contrasts.

Calceolaria
Calceolaria integrifolia
Height: 8–18 in. (20–45 cm); upright, bushy
Blooms: May–September
Grown as an annual

▶ **a classic for cool, coastal areas**

Flowers: Yellow; panicles with roundish, "pocketbook-like" individual flowers. **Growing:** From cuttings, take in August/September, winter over in a bright spot at 41°–50° F (5°–10° C); for varieties propagated by seed, grow in January/February at 59°–68° F (15°–20° C). **Planting:** From mid May, 8–10 in. (20–25 cm) apart. **Care:** High water requirement, fertilize lightly once a week, regularly remove spent flowers; provide protection from rain if possible. **Design:** A popular and attractive combination is with red geraniums (pelargoniums) and blue lobelia or ageratums.

Pot Marigold
Calendula officinalis
Height: 12–18 in. (30–45 cm); upright, bushy
Blooms: May–September
Annual

▶ **choose low pot varieties**

Flowers: Yellow, orange, often with dark centers; single or double, up to 3–4 in. (8–10 cm) Ø. **Growing:** From seed in February or March or sow directly in plant container after April; light-germinator. **Planting:** From beginning of May, 8 in. (20 cm) apart. **Care:** Keep evenly damp, fertilize every 2 weeks, regularly remove spent flowers. **Design:** Attractive in exuberantly colorful summer flower boxes with other yellows as well as with red flowers; also provide harmonizing spots of color beside potted tomatoes and herbs.

GOOD PARTNERS
Petunias, calceolaria, coleus

In a sunny location, these plants need quite a lot of water. If they are in part shade, on the other hand, you should be conservative with the watering.

Fleabane
Erigeron hybrids
Height: 18–32 in. (45–80 cm); erect
Blooms: June–September
Perennial

▶ **beautiful companion perennial**

Flowers: White, pink, violet, and lavender with golden eye; daisylike.
Growing: From seed January to March; light-germinator. **Planting:** From mid May, 8–12 in. (20–30 cm) apart. **Care:** Keep evenly damp, regularly remove spent flowers; after flowering cut back by one-third. **Design:** Goes very well in larger pots with ageratum, heliotrope, and festuca (or ornamental grasses). **Zone:** 4–11.

Geranium
Pelargonium zonale hybrids
Height: 12–20 in. (30–50 cm); upright
Blooms: May–October
Tender perennial, grown as an annual

▶ **the tried-and-true geranium**

Flowers: Red, pink, lavender, white, also bicolored; single or double.
Growing: From cuttings; for varieties grown from seed, sow in December/January (bright, at 60°–77° F [20°–24° C]), prick out twice. **Planting:** From mid May, 8–10 in. (20–25 cm) apart. **Care:** Keep moderately damp but not wet, fertilize biweekly, remove spent flowers; stop fertilizing mid August, bring in to a bright spot before first frost, winter over at 40° F (5° C). **Design:** As dominating lead plant, also can be combined as a companion with plants of many species.

Petunia
Petunia hybrids
Height: 8–15 in. (20–38 cm); upright, cascading
Blooms: May–September
Annual

▶ **some varieties fragrant**

Flowers: All colors, also multicolored; trumpet- or saucer-shaped, large- or small-flowered. **Growing:** From seed from February to March, prick out into individual pots. **Planting:** From mid May, 8–12 in. (20–30 cm) apart. **Care:** Need lots of water, fertilize weekly; remove spent flowers; after first flowering, around the end of July, cut back by half; large-flowered varieties are rain-sensitive. **Design:** Very attractive in purple-white mixtures; striking companions for tall species like tobacco plant, salvia farinacea, geraniums.

CROSS-REFERENCE
Trailing geraniums page 78

CROSS-REFERENCE
Hanging Petunia page 79

Small or Trailing Flowers Tolerating Shade

Ageratum

Ageratum houstonianum
Height: 6–12 in. (15–30 cm); bushy, compact
Blooms: May–October
Grown as an annual

▶ **weatherproof, constant bloomer**

Flowers: Blue, purple, pink, white; corymbose with roundish small flower heads. **Growing:** From seed from February to March. **Planting:** From mid May, 8 in. (20 cm) apart. **Care:** Keep evenly damp, fertilize every 3 weeks, regularly cut off spent flowers. **Design:** Good for foreground plantings in front of taller species in boxes or along the edges of planters.

Snapdragon

Antirrhinum majus
Height: 6–48 in. (15–120 cm); bushy/ trailing
Blooms: June–September
Perennial raised as annual

▶ **exuberantly bright color mixtures**

Flowers: Yellow, pink, red, white; in clusters, with typical "little mouth" form. **Growing:** From seed in March; shorten the center shoot of young plants. **Planting:** Starting in May, 8 in. (20 cm) apart. **Care:** Keep evenly damp, fertilize lightly every 3 weeks. **Design:** With the mixed colors, blue partners like lobelia or dwarf morning glory are very attractive.

Bellflower

Campanula species
Height: 4–36 in. (10–90 cm) upright/ trailing
Blooms: June/July–September
Perennial

▶ **its own special charm**

Flowers: Blue, violet, pink, or white bellflowers. **Growing:** Sow seed-propagated varieties in February/ March. **Planting:** From April, 8–12 in. (20–30 cm) apart. **Care:** Keep evenly damp, fertilize every 4 weeks; cut off stems of spent flowers; winter over bright and above freezing. **Propagating:** Possible by division. **Design:** *C. portenschlagiana* and *C. poscharskyana* (caution, invasive) form runners and can also be used as attractive hanging plants.

GOOD PARTNERS
Marigolds, calceolaria, zinnias

EXPERT TIP
The dwarf variety 'Floral Carpet', with its varied colors, is very beautiful.

EXPERT TIP
Campanula carpatica is suitable for underplanting standards.

In combination with vertical, tall-growing deck or hothouse plants, companions that are low and slightly trailing are the salt in the soup.

Lobelia

Lobelia erinus
Height: 4–8 in. (10–20 cm); bushy/trailing
Blooms: May–August
Perennial raised as annual

▶ **a finishing touch for any planting**

Flowers: Blue, violet, rose, sometimes with white eyes, white; small, very numerous. **Growing:** From seed from February to March, light-germinator; prick out into pots in bunches. **Planting:** From mid May, 8 in. (20 cm) apart. **Care:** Keep evenly damp, fertilize lightly every 3 weeks; after the first flowering (July), cut back by one-third. **Design:** Suitable for a "filler" or front planting along the edges of boxes or saucer planters (trailing form) with almost all summer flowers; also as underplanting for standards.

Sweet Alyssum

Lobularia maritima
Height: 4–8 in. (10–20 cm); cushionlike
Blooms: May–October
Annual

▶ **with a flowery honey fragrance**

Flowers: White, pink, lavender; small, in clusters up to 2 in. (5 cm) long.
Growing: From seed in March/April.
Planting: From mid May, 6 in. (15 cm) apart. **Care:** Keep evenly damp, cut back after first flowering, then fertilize once. **Design:** Attractive "fillers" for edges of boxes, beautiful companions for many upright-growing plants; also for underplantings of hothouse plants or standards.

Cupflower

Nierembergia hippomanica
Height: 6–9 in. (15–22 cm); broad, cushionlike
Blooms: June/July–October
Perennial raised as annual

▶ **robust and weatherproof**

Flowers: Blue, lavender, red, white, with golden-yellow center; saucer- or cup-shaped. **Growing:** From seed in March/April. **Planting:** From mid May, 8 in. (20 cm) apart. **Care:** Keep evenly damp but not wet, fertilize biweekly, regularly remove spent flowers.
Propagating: By cuttings taken in August, winter over bright at about 50° F (10° C); pinch back young plants.
Design: Embellishes saucer planters, boxes, and hanging pots; also as underplanting of standards.

EXPERT TIP
Use long-stemmed trailing forms like 'Sapphire' as hanging plants.

GOOD PARTNERS
Heliotrope, Cape marigolds, geraniums

EXPERT TIP
Good varieties are 'Mont Blanc' (white) and 'Purple Robe' (wine red).

Shade-Lovers

Astilbe, Spirea

Astilbe species

Height: 12–36 in. (30–90 cm); upright, bushy
Blooms: June–September
Perennial

▶ **handsome, decorative pot plants**

Flowers: Red, pink, white, in candle- or plumelike panicles. **Growing:** Sowing and division possible, better to buy young plants. **Planting:** From April, dwarf astilbes, 8–10 in. (20–25 cm) apart. **Care:** Always keep well watered; every spring provide with slow-release fertilizer; winter over outside with winter protection or above freezing, light or dark. **Design:** Put taller varieties in their own separate pots, grouping together plants of different colors. **Zone:** 4–8.

Tuberous-Rooted Begonia

Begonia × *Tuberhybrida*

Height: 6–14 in. (15–35 cm); upright/ trailing
Blooms: May–October
Tuber raised as annual

▶ **strong flower colors**

Flowers: All colors except blue; usually double, up to 5 in. (13 cm) Ø; hanging varieties often small-flowered. **Growing:** Pot up tubers (curved side down) in February/ March, bright at 68° F (20° C), keep moist. **Planting:** After hardening off and after mid May, plant young plants, 8–10 in. (20–25 cm) apart. **Care:** Keep moist (never soggy!); fertilize lightly every 2 weeks, remove spent flowers; it's hardly worth it to winter the tubers over. **Design:** Yellow-orange-red mixtures brighten up dark decks.

Fuchsia

Fuchsia × *hybrida*

Height: 12–36 in. (30–90 cm); upright/ trailing
Blooms: May–October
Perennial treated as annual

▶ **also sun-tolerant varieties**

Flowers: Red, pink, white, also bicolors; tubelike, single or double. **Growing:** From cuttings taken in spring or September; pinch back young plants. **Planting:** From mid May, 8–10 in. (20–25 cm). **Care:** Always keep damp, fertilize weekly until the middle of August, regularly remove spent flowers; wind-protected situation; winter over light or dark at 43° F (6° C). **Design:** For boxes and saucer planters, low varieties like 'Annabel' or 'Cascade'; tall varieties also as potted plants and standards.

EXPERT TIP
'Finale' is an excellent dwarf with light pink flowers.

EXPERT TIP
The hanging begonia 'Giant Cascade Double Mix' has 5-in. flowers.

GOOD PARTNERS
Swedish ivy, impatiens

For balconies with poor light, make use of the multitude of reliably shade-tolerant varieties. Foliage plants like ivy and ferns expand the design possibilities.

Hosta
Hosta species
Height: 12–30 in. (30–76 cm); broad
Blooms: July–August
Perennial

▶ **magnificent leaf variegation**

Flowers: White, lavender; trumpet-shaped in clusters on long stems.
Growing: Buy young plants. **Planting:** From March/April, individually in large pots; mix organic complete fertilizer and perlite into lean transplanting soil.
Care: Keep evenly damp, winter over outside with winter protection or in a frost-free spot inside, bright or dark; later, in spring, provide with slow-release fertilizer. **Propagation:** Division in spring or fall possible. **Design:** Put green-leaved, white- and yellow-edged varieties together. **Zone:** 3–9.

Impatiens, Busy Lizzie
Impatiens hybrids
Height: 8–16 in. (20–40 cm); bushy to spreading
Blooms: May–October
Annual

▶ **don't put outside too early**

Flowers: *Walleriana* hybrids white, rose, pink; 'New Guinea' hybrids also orange, violet; single or double. **Growing:** From seed in February/March.
Planting: End of May, 8–12 in. (20–30 cm) apart. **Care:** Always keep well watered, fertilize lightly every 2 weeks; cut back now and again; set up rain protection; wintering over possible, light at 59° F (15° C). **Propagation:** From cuttings taken in March; pinch back young plants. **Design:** Mixed colors look very attractive in large saucer planters.

Monkey Flower
Mimulus hybrids
Height: 12–18 in. (30–45 cm); bushy
Blooms: June–September
Annual

▶ **also for bright north-facing decks**

Flowers: Yellow, cream, orange, red, brown, often multicolored, sometimes striped or spotted; trumpetlike, large- or small-flowered. **Growing:** From seed from February to April; also possible to sow directly in boxes at the beginning of May; pinch back young plants. **Planting:** From mid May, 6–10 in. (15–25 cm) apart. **Care:** Keep evenly damp, fertilize biweekly; cut back after first flowering. **Design:** Mixed colors like 'Calypso Mixture' and 'Malibu Series' are very attractive.

GOOD PARTNERS
Fuchsias, ferns (in separate pots)

GOOD PARTNERS
Fuchsias, ivy, lobelias

Hanging Pots and Trailing Plants

Brachycome

Brachycome iberidifolin

Stem length: 12–14 in. (30–35 cm); semitrailing, round
Blooms: July–September
Annual

▶ **charming, delicately fragrant**

Flowers: Blue, violet, rose, white, with yellow centers; daisylike. **Growing:** From seed in March/April. **Planting:** From mid May, 8 in. (20 cm) apart. **Care:** Keep evenly damp, fertilize every 3 weeks, regularly remove spent flowers. **Design:** For hanging pots, as underplanting for standards, as trailing plants in the foreground of boxes.

Dwarf Morning Glory

Convolvulus sabatius

Stem length: Up to 39 in. (1 m); semi-trailing
Blooms: May–October
Perennial grown as an annual

▶ **silvery green leaves**

Flowers: Blue, violet; trumpet-shaped. **Growing:** From seed in March. **Planting:** From mid May, 8–10 in. (20–25 cm) apart. **Care:** Always keep slightly damp, fertilize every 2 weeks until the middle of August, cut back stems that have finished flowering; winter over at 50° C (10° C), shortening the stems by a good half beforehand. **Propagating:** By stem cuttings from fall to spring. **Design:** Is lovely as a hanging plant when combined with Mediterranean hothouse plants; also as a compatible companion in mixed boxes.

Hanging Geranium

Pelargonium peltatum hybrids

Stem length: up to 59 in. (150 cm)
Blooms: May–October
Perennial grown as an annual

▶ **robust and free-flowering**

Flowers: Red, rose, lavender, white, also bicolored; single or double. **Growing:** Sow seed-propagated varieties in January/February, bright, at 68–75° F (20–24° C), prick out twice. **Planting:** From mid May, 8–12 in. (20–30 cm) apart. **Care:** Keep evenly damp but not wet, fertilize biweekly, remove spent flowers; stop fertilizing mid August; before frost, move to a bright spot, winter over at 41° F (5° C). **Propagating:** By cuttings in late summer. **Design:** Can be combined with almost all deck flowers, in boxes or hanging pots or baskets.

GOOD PARTNERS
Browallia, geraniums, Dahlberg daisies

EXPERT TIP
Some varieties are self-cleaning.

So-called "self-cleaning" plants drop their spent flowers of their own accord. This is an especially useful characteristic in hanging plants.

Hanging Petunia
Petunia hybrids
Stem length: 10–59 in. (25–150 cm)
Blooms: May–October
Annual

▶ **overwhelmingly floriferous**

Flowers: All colors, also multicolored; large (grandiflora) or small trumpet-shaped flowers (multiflora). **Growing:** Difficult, best to buy young plants. **Planting:** From mid May, 8–12 in. (20–30 cm) apart. **Care:** High water requirement, fertilize biweekly; modern varieties are weatherproof, must be neither deadheaded nor cut back. **Design:** The vigorously growing multifloras should only be combined with similar partners; the 'Wave' series are excellent in containers.

Fanflower
Scaevola saligna
Stem length: up to 39 in. (1 m); semi-trailing
Flowers: May–October
Annual

▶ **undemanding, long-flowering**

Flowers: Violet, blue; like small fans. **Growing:** Best to buy young plants or take cuttings in fall. **Planting:** From mid May, 8 in. (20 cm) apart. **Care:** Keep evenly damp, fertilize lightly biweekly; self-cleaning; wintering over (bright, 59° F [15° C]) possible. **Propagating:** From cuttings taken in fall or spring. **Design:** Spreading growth as spreading specimen hanging plant; in mixed plantings, a compatible companion plant for edges of container.

Knotweed, Fleeceflower
Polygonum capitatum
Stem length: 12 in. (20 cm) or more; spreading
Blooms: June–September
Annual

▶ **an extremely fast grower**

Flowers: White and pink; small spikes. **Growing:** Start seeds 4–6 weeks before last frost. **Planting:** Full sun to light shade, plant after last frost, about 8–12 in. (20–30 cm) apart. **Care:** Fertilize lightly every 3 weeks. **Design:** For hanging containers, good for an edging plant that will trail over; compliments blue-flowered companion plants.

GOOD PARTNERS
Geranium marigold, fanflower, verbena, licorice plant, cape marigold

GOOD PARTNERS
Geraniums, pinks, daisies

Annual Vines

Vines for Sunny Spots

Name	Height Growth Form	Flower Color In Bloom
Maurandya, twining snapdragon (*Asarina barclaiana*)	up to 10 ft (3 m) creeper	rose, violet, blue June–October
Balloon vine, heart pea, winter cherry (*Cardiospermum halicacabum*)	up to 10 ft (3 m) creeper	green/ornamental fruits June–August
Summer squash (*Cucurbita pepo*)	up to 13 ft (4 m) creeper	yellow/ornamental fruits June–September
Chilean glory vine, glory flower (*Eccremocarpus scaber*)	up to 10 ft (3 m) creeper	red, orange July–September
White-flowered gourd, calabash gourd (*Lagenaria siceraria*)	up to 13 ft (4 m) creeper	white/ornamental fruits July–September
Pharbitis (*Ipomoea purpurea*)	up to 10 ft (3 m) twiner	blue, red, rose July–September
Cypress vine, star-glory (*Quamoclit pinnata*)	up to 25 ft (8 m) twiner	white-red June–September
Purple bell vine (*Rhodochiton atrosanguineus*)	up to 10 ft (3 m) twiner	red, violet June–October

Vines for Sun/Part Shade

Climbing fumatory, mountain-fringe, Alleghany vine (*Adlumia fungosa*)	up to 7 ft (2 m) creeper	rose June–August
Scarlet runner bean (*Phaseolus coccineus*)	up to 10 ft (3 m) twiner	white, red June–September
Canary-bird flower, canary creeper (*Tropaeolum peregrinum*)	up to 10 ft (3 m) creeper	yellow, orange, red July–October

Cathedral Bells, Cup-and-Saucer Vine, Mexican Ivy
Cobaea scandens
Height: up to 25 ft (8 m); creeping
Blooms: July–October
Tender perennial grown as an annual

▶ **enchanting privacy screen**

Flowers: Violet, red, blue, white; bell-shaped, up to 3 in. (8 cm) long. **Growing:** In March, put two seeds on end in each pot. **Planting:** From mid May, 20–24 in. (50–60 cm) apart. **Care:** Needs much water, fertilize every 2 weeks; better branching if tips of shoots are pinched back. **Design:** Fast-growing in sufficiently large pots; attractive arrangement: violet and white varieties, in separate pots to left and right of deck or entrance door, allowed to grow together at the top. **Zone:** 9.

Common Hops
Humulus lupulus
Height: up to 13 ft (4 m); stem twiner
Blooms: July/August
Annual, perennial in Zones 6–9

▶ **decorative foliage**

Ornamentation: Sturdy green, lobed, large leaves, white-streaked in 'Variegata'; flowers insignificant. **Growing:** From seed in February/March, pricked out into individual pots. **Planting:** From mid-May, 16–20 in. (40–50 cm) apart. **Care:** Needs much water, fertilize every 8 weeks. **Design:** After very few weeks provides dense protection from view and wind, depending on density of planting; also suitable for north sides.

EXPERT TIP
All climbing plants need training stakes, even in their first pots.

**Creepers climb best on wire or
trellises, twiners like to twine up stakes,
vertical wires, or strings.**

Morning Glory
Ipomoea tricolor
Height: Up to 10 ft (3 m); twiner
Blooms: July–October
Perennial raised as annual

▶ **distinctive giant flowers**
Flowers: Blue, red, white throats; up
to 5 in. (13 cm) Ø; close in the after-
noons. **Growing:** From seed in
March/April, prick out into individual
pots. **Planting:** From mid May, 12–16
in. (30–40 cm) apart. **Care:** Keep well
moistened at all times but not wet;
fertilize biweekly; position as protected from wind and rain as possible. **Design:** With black-eyed Susan vine or
cypress vine in separate pots, you
have a very attractive wall of flowers.

Sweet Pea
Lathyrus odoratus
Height: up to 7 ft (2 m); creeper
Blooms: June–September
Annual

▶ **also bushy varieties**
Flowers: Rose, white, red, lavender;
up to 2½ in. (6 cm) across; in loose
clusters. **Growing:** From seed in
March/April, 3–4 seeds per pot; also
sowing directly in container possible
from mid April. **Planting:** From mid
May, 8–12 in. (20–30 cm) apart. **Care:**
Keep evenly damp, fertilize biweekly;
regularly remove spent flowers; wind-
protected location. **Design:** Frequently
available as bright or pastel mixtures;
bushy varieties (12–16 in. [20–40 cm]
high) also suitable for mixed boxes.

Black-Eyed Susan Vine
Thunbergia alata
Height: up to 5 ft (1.5 m); twiner
Blooms: June–October
Perennial raised as annual

▶ **usefully versatile**
Flowers: Yellow, orange, white, usually with a black eye; up to 2 in. (5 cm)
Ø. **Growing:** From seed from February
to March, 3–4 seeds per pot; pinch
back young plants. **Planting:** From mid
May, 8–16 in. (20–40 cm) apart. **Care:**
Keep evenly damp, fertilize every 3
weeks; site in a spot as protected from
wind and rain as possible. **Design:** Also cuts a good figure in hanging pots
and mixed boxes; in a pot set up high,
very charming as a half-climbing, half-
trailing plant.

EXPERT TIP
*For the best fragrance, select
older varieties, such as 'Painted Lady'.*

Late Bloomers,

Decorative Leaves

**The transition from fall
to winter planting is often fleeting.
Plant containers for late-season combinations
must be completely frost-proof.**

Many summer flowers bloom bravely into October, but the first casualties start to appear as early as September—admittedly, too, the enthusiasm for maintaining the deck or patio slackens. Dreary late-season days weigh far less on the spirits if there is something green, or even flowering, outside the window.

Growth Predictions

Fall and winter bloomers can of course be gradually inserted in the gaps left behind by the summer flowers, but specially prepared plant containers are better suited to the purpose. With most of the late-bloomers it's a matter of winter-hardy perennials. Bought in fall as small seasonal plants, they can be placed quite close together in boxes, since they hardly grow at all during the cold season. But if you want to keep the plants growing afterwards, you should repot them into larger containers the second spring after buying them. There they generally develop into handsome plants that you can combine, with very few

exceptions, in one and the same container with other plants.

Furthermore, nurseries and mail-order houses are increasingly offering collections of plants for fall and winter. If you have only a little experience, this is a recommended way to go. It will give you a good foundation for being able to try out your own arrangements eventually.

Ornamental Leaves—Not Only in Fall

As the number of possible flower choices dwindles, plants with ornamental foliage like bergenia or Dusty Miller or various grasses and ferns come increasingly to the fore. Ornamental foliage is not only decorative in fall and winter, however, but is also valuable for offsetting the bright colors of summer flowers or to provide special accents. Some of these plants are also suitable for semishady to shady spots and also may have aromatic scents.

Fall enchantment on the deck: delicate flowers, colorful foliage, ornamental fruit, and variegated leaves.

Fall- and Winter-Bloomers

New England Aster
Aster novae-anglial
Height: 1–3 ft (30 cm–1 m); upright, compact
Blooms: September–October
Perennial

► **buy special deck asters**

Flowers: All colors except yellow; numerous. **Planting:** Set out purchased plants in August/September, 8–12 in. (20–30 cm) apart. **Care:** Keep moderately damp; after wintering over (bright, above freezing or with winter protection), provide with slow-release fertilizer in spring; fertilize as necessary during summer. **Propagating:** Possible through division in spring. **Design:** Blue and white varieties are especially valuable, since they buffer the numerous pink and red shades of fall. **Zone:** 3–8.

Scotch Heather
Calluna vulgaris
Height: 8–24 in. (20–60 cm); upright/creeping
Blooms: July–December
Dwarf evergreen shrub

► **many color nuances**

Flowers: Rose, white, red, violet; little bells, dense and numerous in clusters. **Planting:** In summer or early fall, 10–18 in. (25–45 cm) apart; in azalea soil mixed with sand. **Care:** Keep evenly damp; can be wintered over outdoors without protection; in spring provide with organic fertilizer or rhododendron fertilizer, fertilize once more in May/June if necessary. **Design:** As a newly bought seasonal plant, a delicate companion; after several years of culture eventually spreads quite wide and dominates. **Zone:** 5–7.

Autumn Crocus
Colchicum hybrids
Height: 4–10 in. (10–25 cm); flowers without leaves
Blooms: August–October
Corm

► **plant in small groups**

Flowers: Rose, violet, white; single or double, small- or large-flowered. **Planting:** Plant tubers in July or August 4–6 in. (10–15 cm) deep or set out purchased plants; 6–8 in. (15–20 cm) apart. **Care:** Keep uniformly damp (never soggy); winter over at above freezing and dark, also outside, with winter protection; from sprouting in spring until June fertilize every 3 weeks, not while flowering. **Design:** Beautiful in large saucer planters with Scotch heather and other fall plants, tone on tone; as an underplanting with potted shrubs. **Zone:** 4–9.

EXPERT TIP
Careful: The plant is very poisonous!

When the first night frosts threaten, it is advisable to protect flowers, especially fall chrysanthemums, with a cover of bubble wrap or row fabric.

Fall Chrysanthemum

Dendranthema grandiflorum hybrids
Height: 10–36 in. (25–90 cm); bushy, branching
Blooms: September–November
Perennial raised as annual

▶ **choose low-growing varieties**

Flowers: All colors except blue; single, double or pom-pomlike, large- or small-flowered. **Planting:** In August/September, 8–12 in. (20–30 cm) apart. **Care:** Keep uniformly damp, fertilize after all flowers have come out; wintering over doesn't pay. **Design:** Very decorative when mixed colorfully in large saucer planters; especially good partners are white Scotch heather and color-coordinated cushion asters.

Alpine Heath

Erica carnea
Height: 6–14 in. (15–35 cm); cushion-like
Blooms: December–April
Dwarf evergreen shrub

▶ **outstandingly winter hardy**

Flowers: Rose, white, red, violet; little bells, dense and numerous in clusters. **Planting:** In September/October, 12 in. (30 cm) apart; in rhododendron or azalea soil mixed with sand. **Care:** Keep evenly damp; can be wintered over outside without protection; in spring provide with organic fertilizer or rhododendron fertilizer, repeating if necessary once to twice more from May to the middle of August. **Design:** Valuable winter bloomer, colorful eye-catcher between dwarf conifers and small evergreen shrubs. **Zone:** 5–8.

Sedum

Sedum spectabile
Height: 18–24 in. (45–60 cm); upright, bushy
Blooms: August–October
Perennial

▶ **beautiful variety: 'Autumn Joy'**

Flowers: Rose; in large umbels. **Planting:** Set out container plants in summer, 12–16 in. (30–40 cm) apart. **Care:** Keep moderately damp, provide with slow-release fertilizer at planting, fertilize after wintering over (bright, above freezing or with winter protection), then every 4 weeks from spring to August; cut back after flowering is finished in fall or spring. **Propagating:** By cuttings taken in early spring/early summer or division in spring. **Design:** Individually in pots, also with low-growing fall flowers and ornamental grasses. **Zone:** 3–11.

EXPERT TIP
Often sold under the name Chrysanthemum

EXPERT TIP
Water heathers and heaths even in winter on above-freezing days.

EXPERT TIP
Sedum 'Ruby Glow', 12 in. (30 cm), is a good choice for containers.

Beautiful Foliage Plants

Sun-Loving Foliage Plants

Name	Growth Habit	Foliage Colors
Blue fescue (*Festuca cinerea*)	8 in. (20 cm) or more clump	frosted blue
Oregano, pot marjoram (*Origanum vulgare* 'Aureum')	bushy to trailing	yellow-green
Ornamental sage (*Salvia officinalis* varieties)	bushy, up to 18 in. (45 cm) tall	yellow-green, white-green, reddish, multicolored
Santolina (*Santolina* species in varieties)	bushy, up 12–24 in. (30–60 cm) tall	silvery
Germander (*Teucrium* species in varieties)	bushy, up to 12 in. (30 cm) tall	green, silvery green

Shade-Tolerant Foliage Plants

Name	Growth Habit	Foliage Colors
Grassy-leaved sweet flag (*Acorus gramineus* varieties)	upright blades, up to 16 in. (40 cm) tall	yellow-green, reddish
Carpet bugleweed (*Ajuga reptans* varieties)	6–9 in. (15–22 cm), trailing	dark-red, green-red, variegated
Sedges (*Carex species in* varieties)	arching	yellow-green, yellow-white
Ground-ivy (*Glechoma hederacea* 'Variegata')	trailing, stems up to 7 ft (2 m) long	green-white
Dead nettle (*Lamium aureum* varieties)	creeping, trailing	silvery-green, yellow-green
Yellow archangel (*Lamiastrum galeobdolon* varieties)	creeping, trailing	silvery-green, yellow-green
Moneywort, creeping Charlie, creeping Jenny (*Lysimachia nummularia* 'Goldilocks')	creeping, trailing	yellow-green

Bergenia

Bergenia cordifolia, Bergenia hybrids
Height: 8–20 in. (20–50 cm); broad, bushy
Blooms: March–May
Perennial

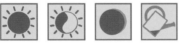

▶ **spring flowers and decorative foliage**

Ornamentation: Green or dark-red leaves, also throughout winter; pink or white bell flowers in large cymes.
Planting: From May/June, for seasonal plantings in fall. **Care:** Keep only slightly damp; winter over outdoors, with winter protection in exposed locations; provide with organic fertilizer or slow-release fertilizer in spring.
Propagating: May be divided after flowering. **Design:** Small plants 10 in. (25 cm) apart in mixed fall plantings, larger ones as specimens or in groups in troughs. **Zone:** 3–8.

Coleus, Painted Nettle

Coleus × hybridus
Height: 8–16 in. (20–40 cm); bushy
Blooms: not applicable
Perennial raised as annual

▶ **best colors in part shade**

Ornamentation: Red-green, red-green-black leaf markings; various patterns depending on variety. **Growing:** From seed in March/April. **Planting:** From mid May, 8–10 in. (20–25 cm) apart. **Care:** Keep evenly damp, fertilize every 2 weeks; immediately break off any flower panicles when they appear.
Propagating: Cuttings taken in fall root easily, winter over bright and cool. **Design:** Combine according to taste with striking red or yellow flowers or pair with discreet blue.

EXPERT TIP
Good for decks are 'Bressingham Ruby' and 'Evening Glow'.

GOOD PARTNERS
Wax begonias, lobelia, Swan River daisies

With trailing forms, in particular, we also speak of "structuring plants." Doing without them in hanging pots and baskets is hardly possible to imagine.

Licorice Plant
Helichrysum petiolare
Height: Stems up to 20 in. (50 cm); semitrailing
Blooms: not applicable
Perennial raised as annual

▶ **adds a silvery accent**

Ornamentation: Leaflets silvery white ('Silver') or green-yellow ('Rondello', 'Aureum'). **Planting:** Set out purchased young plants after the middle of May, 8–10 in. (20–25 cm) apart. **Care:** Keep evenly damp; fertilize biweekly. **Propagating:** From cuttings taken in summer. **Design:** For hanging pots and baskets and mixed boxes; marvelously underlines the flowers of strongly growing partners like hanging verbenas, fanflowers, petunias, marigolds.

Swedish Ivy
Plectranthus coleoides
Height: Stem length up to 7 ft (2 m); trailing
Blooms: August/September
Perennial raised as annual

▶ **variegated forms available**

Ornamentation: White- or yellow-edged leaves; flowers insignificant. **Planting:** From mid May, 8–12 in. (20–30 cm) apart. **Care:** Keep moderately damp, fertilize every 2 weeks until the middle of August; overwintering possible (bright, at 50° F [10° C]). **Propagating:** From cuttings taken in March/April, pinch back young plants. **Design:** Beautiful, although very vigorous, companion for many summer and fall flowers like geraniums, fuchsias, chrysanthemums; also very effective by itself in decorative plant containers.

Dusty Miller
Senecio bicolor
Height: 8–12 in. (20–30 cm); upright, broad
Blooms: not applicable
Annual

▶ **very elegant effect**

Ornamentation: White- or greenish-silver, lobed or deeply segmented leaves; countless forms as well as varieties. **Growing:** From seed from January to March. **Planting:** From mid May or in late summer, 8–12 in. (20–30 cm) apart. **Care:** Keep only slightly damp, fertilize lightly every 2 weeks; place where protected from rain. **Design:** Quiet spot between colorful plantings and color mixtures but also in reserved pink-blue-white combinations.

EXPERT TIP
Other names: Swedish begonia, prostrate coleus, spur flower

GOOD PARTNERS
Petunias, marigolds, lobelias

Ornamental Shrubs

for Deck and Patio

Fall, winter, shade—where summer flowers don't grow, shrubs reveal their special strengths. Among them are spring flowers and walls of green, and many more.

As "permanent plants" the shrubs introduced here can remain outside all year-round, often without any winter protection. In regions with frosty winters, however, it's advisable to lay Styrofoam sheets under the pots and wrap them, since the soil in pots freezes solid relatively quickly.

Of Dwarves and Giants

The small conifers are among the most common shrubs for containers. They are prime illustrators of all the things that can be done with shrubs. Although some of these "dwarf" varieties can eventually grow up to 7 ft (2 m) tall and wide, you often find them in mixed permanent plantings—as many as four or five in a 3-ft (1-m) box! This works because they grow extremely slowly and, in addition, the narrow space for their roots limits their growth. Many broad-leaved evergreens behave similarly, even though they usually attain size more quickly. Therefore, don't be frightened off by the top sizes in the portraits: These sizes are only reached after sev-

eral years. And then there is always the possibility of giving it to a friend with a garden—or swapping it for a smaller shrub.

Plant Stock and Containers

Preferably, you should buy container plants that have already been raised in plastic pots. Although they can be planted at any time of the year, spring is the most favorable time. Then the new acquisitions can grow well until winter. The planting containers must be of frost-proof material and, for larger shrubs, really roomy: diameters of 20–24 in. (50–60 cm) diameter or width and height of 16 in. (40 cm) at the very least. Tubs for trellis plants should hold at least 20 qt. (20 L) of soil. Very important: large drainage holes and a drainage layer over them, for example of perlite. The soil mix— single-purpose soil or good deck soil mixed with sand—should be changed every 3 years.

Ornamental shrubs and vines provide a "green framework" on deck and patio all year-round.

Small Flowering Shrubs

Flowering Shrubs for Pot Culture

Name	Flower Color Blooming Period	Height Special Features
Serviceberry (*Amelanchier lamarckii*)	white April–May	up to 7 ft (2 m) fruits, fall color
Bluebeard, blue spirea (*Caryopteris* x *clandonensis*)	blue September–October	up to 39 in. (1 m)
Rose daphne (*Daphne cneorum*)	pink April–May	up to 16 in. (0.4 m) poisonous!
Witch hazel (*Hamamelis* species)	yellow January–March	up to 7 ft (2 m) fall color
Saint-John's-wort (*Hypericum* species)	yellow July–September	20–39 in. (0.5–1 m) shade-tolerant
Lavender (*Lavandula angustifolia*)	blue, violet, white June–August	up to 24 in. (0.6 m) fragrant subshrub
Star magnolia (*Magnolia stellata*)	white March–April	5–7 ft (1.5–2 m) fragrant
Flowering crab (*Malus* varieties)	White, pink May–June	up to 7 ft (2 m)
Weeping pussy willow (*Salix caprea* 'Pendula')	yellow, silvery March–April	up to 5 ft (1.5 m) standard
Spirea (*Spiraea* species)	white, pink April/May, June/July	16–32 in. (0.4–0.8 m)
Littleleaf lilac (*Syringa microphylla*)	pink June–September	up to 7 ft (2 m) fragrant
Viburnum (*Viburnum farreri*)	white March–April	up to 7 ft (2 m) fragrant

Broom
Cytisus species
Height: 8–24 in. (20–60 cm); bushy/creeping
Blooms: April–June
Deciduous small shrub

▶ **usually broadly spreading**

Flowers: Yellow, in *C. purpureus* crimson-rose. **Planting:** In spring, plant in wide pots or trough planters. **Care:** Keep only very slightly damp; fertilize little; as flowering falls off, cut back a portion of the shoots hard; winter over outside, with protection if necessary. **Propagating:** By cuttings taken after flowering. **Design:** Plants that are still small can be paired with suitable partners like dwarf conifers and heaths. **Zone:** 6–8.

Shrubby Cinquefoil
Potentilla fruticosa
Height: Up to 3 ft (1 m); broadly bushy
Blooms: May–October
Deciduous small shrub

▶ **robust ever-bloomer**

Flowers: Yellow, white, or pink saucer flowers, up to 1 in. (3 cm) Ø. **Planting:** In spring, individually in pots. **Care:** Keep moderately damp; fertilize every 4 weeks until mid August; winter over outside, with winter protection as needed; tolerates severe pruning. **Propagating:** Through semiwoody cuttings, taken in summer. **Design:** Small, late-blooming cultivars are still available in September for fall plantings; for instance, can be combined with Scotch heather and dwarf conifers. **Zone:** 3–8.

**Bear in mind your deck's weight tolerances—
big pots are required for the taller shrubs and they are
heavy, especially right after watering!**

Flowering Cherry
Prunus species and varieties
Height: up to 3 ft (2 m); bushy
Blooms: April–May
Deciduous shrub

▶ lush spring bloomer

Flowers: Depending on variety, white or pink, in different shadings, single or double, up to 2½ in. (3 cm) Ø.
Planting: In early spring in large, stable containers. **Care:** Keep moderately damp; fertilize weekly in spring and summer; winter over outside, if necessary with slight frost protection, water a little on above-freezing days, do not allow to dry out; cut back in spring.
Design: As a specimen or standard with underplanting. **Zone:** 4–8.

Rhododendron
Rhododendron hybrids
Height: 20–39 in. (50–100 cm); broadly bushy
Blooms: April–June
Evergreen shrub

▶ preferably in part shade

Flowers: Red, rose, white, lavender, yellow; large clusters. **Planting:** In May or early fall in pots with rhododendron soil. **Care:** In spring/summer water copiously, keep slightly damp the rest of the year (use softened water!); apply rhododendron fertilizer three times from April to June; break off spent flower stalks; protect from wind; winter over outside, with protection if needed. **Design:** *Forrestii* and *Yakushimanum* hybrids individually in tubs, smaller Korean azaleas also in boxes. **Zone:** 5–8.

Roses
Rosa species and varieties
Height: 12–59 in. (30–150 cm); bushy/creeping
Blooms: June–October
Deciduous shrub

▶ only a few miniature roses are fragrant

Flowers: All colors except blue, usually double. **Planting:** Container plants from April to June; miniature roses at 10 in. (25 cm) apart, larger varieties alone. **Care:** Keep moderately damp; fertilize weekly until the end of July; cut off withered rose stalks; winter over above freezing, dark or outside with good protection; cut back in spring. **Design:** For planters, low bedding roses, tree roses, ground-cover roses; miniature or pot-roses also in groups in flower boxes. **Zone:** 4–9.

GOOD PARTNERS
Underplanting in spring with tulips, hyacinths, narcissi

EXPERT TIP
Since they are very sensitive to lime, use only special soils and fertilizers.

EXPERT TIP
Do not place directly in front of a bright house wall (risk of trapped heat).

Broad-Leaved Evergreens

Barberry
Berberis species
Height: 16–32 in. (40–80 cm); broadly bushy
Blooms: May
Evergreen small shrub

▶ **paleleaf barberries also for shade**

Ornamentation: Dark green leaflets all year round; beautiful growth form: Magellan barberry (*B. buxifolia* 'Nana') roundish, paleleaf barberry (*B. candidula*) slightly arching and yellow-flowered. **Planting:** In spring in wide pots or troughs. **Care:** Keep moderately damp; until the middle of August, fertilize every 4 weeks; winter over outdoors, with protection as needed; tolerates pruning well. **Propagating:** By cuttings taken in fall. **Design:** Combinations with other plants possible in large containers. **Zone:** 4–8.

Boxwood
Buxus sempervirens 'Suffruticosa'
Height: up to 39 in. (1 m); densely bushy
Blooms: April–May
Evergreen small shrub

▶ **can be pruned into various shapes**

Ornamentation: Glossy, dark green leaflets all year round, flowers small, yellow, fragrant. **Planting:** In spring in large pots. **Care:** Keep moderately moist; fertilize every 4 weeks until the middle of August; winter over outside, with winter protection if needed; best pruning time end of May and August. **Propagating:** By cuttings taken in early summer. **Design:** Can be pruned into almost any desired shape; rounded box spheres are prettiest in terracotta pots. **Zone:** 6–9.

Wintergreen
Gaultheria procumbens
Height: up to 8 in. (0.2 m); flat, spreading
Blooms: June–July
Dwarf evergreen shrub

▶ **red-fruited carpet**

Ornamentation: Red, round, berrylike fruits beginning in September; pinkish white clusters of flowers; dark green leaflets. **Planting:** In spring or fall in rhododendron soil. **Care:** Keep only slightly damp (softened water); apply rhododendron fertilizer every 8 weeks until August; winter over outside, with winter protection if necessary; prune away offending shoots only. **Design:** A beautiful companion plant for other dwarf shrubs in large boxes or planter. **Zone:** 3–8.

EXPERT TIP
Caution, the paleleaf barberry (B. candidula) is very thorny.

GOOD PARTNERS
Rhododendron, Scotch heather, heath, dwarf pines

**All shrubs—especially the evergreens—
need watering from time to time during the winter. It's best
to place them in a shady spot until spring.**

Pernettya

Pernettya mucronata
Height: up to 32 in. (0.8 m); broadly bushy
Blooms: May–June
Evergreen small shrub

▶ **lime-sensitive, shade-loving**

Ornamentation: Starting in fall, numerous round berries, red, pink, or white; flowers insignificant. **Planting:** In spring or fall in rhododendron soil. **Care:** Keep evenly damp (use softened water); until August apply rhododendron fertilizer every 8 weeks; winter over outside with good protection; cut away offending shoots only. **Design:** Plantings and partners similar to wintergreen and skimmia; especially charming: variety 'Alba' with large, white berries. **Zone:** 5–8.

Cherry Laurel

Prunus laurocerasus varieties
Height: 3–10 ft (1–3 m); upright or spreading
Blooms: May
Evergreen shrub

▶ **very shade tolerant**

Ornamentation: Up to 6-in.- (15-cm-) long, dark green, glossy leaves all year-round; white flower candles up to 4 in. (10 cm) high. **Planting:** In spring in large pots. **Care:** Water moderately, copiously if location is sunny, fertilize every 4 weeks until August; winter over outside, with winter protection as needed; tolerates pruning, even hard cutting back is possible. **Propagating:** By cuttings taken in fall. **Design:** Very decorative specimen plant. **Zone:** 6–9.

Japanese Skimmia

Skimmia japonica
Height: up to 3–4 ft. (1–1¼ m); broad, compact
Blooms: April
Dwarf evergreen shrub

▶ **fruits into spring**

Ornamentation: Long-lasting red, round fruits in fall, white flower panicles, large, decorative leaves. **Planting:** In spring or fall. **Care:** Always keep well dampened; fertilize every 4 weeks until the middle of August; winter over outside, with winter protection as needed; prune only offending branches. **Propagating:** By cuttings in fall. **Design:** Excellent in permanent plantings with dwarf conifers, Scotch heather, and small rhododendrons. **Zone:** 6–8.

▶ **EXPERT TIP**
Protect from night frosts with sacking or row fabric.

▶ **EXPERT TIP**
Male plants do not bear fruit; only buy plants marked "fruiting variety."

Dwarf Conifers

Dwarf Balsam Fir
Abies balsamea 'Nana'
Height/Width: 12–16 in.
(30–40 cm)/16–24 in. (40–60 cm)
Growth habit: flat spherical, wide
Dwarf evergreen shrub

▶ **do not place in front of a south wall**

Needles: Dark green above, two white stripes below, up to ½ in. (1.5 cm) long, close together; slightly fragrant. **Planting:** In spring or fall, in troughs or large saucer planters. **Care:** Keep moderately damp; in spring apply slow-release fertilizer, fertilize again in June with conifer fertilizer; heat-sensitive; winter over outside, with protection as needed. **Other varieties:** Alpine fir *A. lasiocarpa* 'Compacta', conical, 24 in. (60 cm), blue-green; for trough plantings. **Zone:** 3–6.

Japanese or Sawara Falsecypress
Chamaecyparis pisifera 'Filifera Aurea'
Height/Width: 20–24 in. (50–60 cm)/12–18 in. (30–40 cm)
Growth habit: globe-shaped
Dwarf evergreen shrub

▶ **overwhelming variety of species and varieties**

Needles: Golden yellow on thin, threadlike, trailing branches. **Planting:** In spring or fall, in troughs or mixed boxes. **Care:** Keep uniformly moist; in spring apply slow-release fertilizer, in June/July fertilize again; heat-sensitive; winter over outside, provide winter protection for containers as necessary. **Other varieties:** *C. pisifera* 'Nana' (mounding), 'Sungold' (yellow-green); *C. lawsoniana* 'Elwoodii' (globe-shaped, upright), 'Minima Glauca' (roundish, blue-green); *C. obtusa* 'Nana Gracilis' (spherical). **Zone:** 4–8.

Dwarf Juniper
Juniperus squamata 'Blue Star'
Height/Width: 8–36 in.
(20–90 cm)/20–24 in. (50–60 cm)
Growth habit: low mounding, very branched
Dwarf evergreen shrub

▶ **atractive blue-needled variety**

Needles: Silvery blue, very close together and very fine, sharp. **Planting:** In spring and fall, in troughs or mixed boxes. **Care:** Keep uniformly damp; apply slow-release fertilizer in spring, again in June/July; winter over outside, provide winter protection for containers as necessary. **Other varieties:** *J. chinensis* 'Pfitzeriana Aurea' (yellow, bushy); *J. communis* 'Meyer' (silvery green, columnar), 'Compressa' (silvery green, broad, cushionlike). **Zone:** 4–7.

EXPERT TIP
Fertilize all needle-leaved shrubs chiefly with conifer fertilizers.

GOOD PARTNERS
In winter red Scotch heather, in summer potted roses

The size measurements are approximate values after 3–5 years of pot culture. With conifers they greatly depend on the dimensions of the plant at the time of purchase.

Dwarf Alberta Spruce
Picea glauca 'Conica'
Height/Width: 12–20 in. (30–50 cm)/
8–16 in. (20–40 cm)
Growth habit: Conical
Dwarf evergreen shrub

▶ **grows very slowly**

Needles: Bluish green, up to ¼ in. (1 cm) long, loosely spaced. **Planting:** In spring or fall, in troughs or mixed boxes. **Care:** Keep moist, water copiously in heat; apply slow-release fertilizer in spring and again in June/July; lightly shaded location preferable; winter over outside, with winter protection for containers as needed. **Other varieties:** *P. abies* 'Little Gem' (green, tight globe); *P. glauca* 'Echiniformis' (blue-green, mounding), *P. omorika* 'Nana' (green, globe-shaped); *P. pungens glauca* 'Globosa' (silvery blue, mounding). **Zone:** 2–6.

Dwarf Mugo Pine
Pinus mugo var. *mugo*
Height/Width: 8–16 in. (20–40 cm)/
16–24 in. (40–60 cm)
Growth habit: mounding to globe-shaped
Dwarf evergreen shrub

▶ **grows very slowly**

Needles: Dark green, up to 4 cm long, in bunches. **Planting:** In spring or fall, in troughs or mixed boxes. **Care:** Keep evenly damp; apply slow-release fertilizer in spring and again in June/July; winter over outside, providing winter protection for containers as needed.
Other varieties: *P. mugo* 'Gnom', 'Humpy' (see picture), 'Mops', 'Mini Mops' var. *pumilio*; *P. densiflora* 'Kobold' (green, globe-shaped); *P. pumila* 'Glauca' (blue-green, broadly bushy). **Zone:** 2–7.

Dwarf Arborvitae
Thuja occidentalis 'Danica'
Height/Width: 8–16 in. (20–40 cm)/
8–16 in. (20–40 cm)
Growth habit: globe-shaped
Dwarf evergreen shrub

▶ **somewhat heat-sensitive**

Needles: Fresh green, in winter slightly brownish green, arranged scalelike. **Planting:** In spring or fall, in troughs or mixed boxes. **Care:** Keep uniformly damp; apply slow-release fertilizer in spring and again in June/July; most rain-protected location possible; winter over outside with winter protection for container as needed.
Other varieties: *T. occidentalis* 'Hetz Midget' (green, globe-shaped), 'Rheingold' (yellow, conical), 'Little Gem' (green, globe-shaped), 'Tiny Tim' (green, globe-shaped). **Zone:** 2–7.

EXPERT TIP
Do not place in front of a hot south wall (increased risk of spider mites!).

EXPERT TIP
The dwarf mugo pines also go very well with perennial herbs.

Woody Vines

Woody Vines for Sunny Locations

Name	Height Growth Habit	Flower Color Blooming Season
Bower vine (*Actinidia arguta*)	up to 20 ft + (6 m) twining	white June–July
Trumpet vine (*Campsis radicans*)	up to 15 ft + (4.5 m) aerial roots	orange, yellow July–September
Wine grape (*Vitis vinifera* ssp. *vinifera*)	up to 10 ft (3 m) tendril-climbing	flowers insignificant, decorative leaves, bunches of grapes
Wisteria (*Wisteria sinensis*)	up to 16 ft (5 m) twining	blue May–June

Woody Vines for Sun/Part Shade

Small-flowered clematis (*Clematis texensis*)	up to 7 ft (2 m) tendril-climbing	scarlet June–September
Large-flowered clematis varieties (*Clematis* hybrids)	up to 10 ft (3 m) tendril-climbing	many colors June–September
Euonymus (*Euonymus fortunei* var. *radicans*)	up to 10 ft (3 m) aerial roots	flowers insignificant, green-variegated leaves
Henry honeysuckle (*Lonicera henryi*)	up to 20 ft (6 m) twining	yellow-red June–July
Virginia creeper (*Parthenocissus quinquefolia*)	up to 20 ft + (6 m) adhesive disks	flowers insignificant, red fall coloring

Dutchman's Pipe
Aristolochia durior
Height: up to 30 ft (9 m); twiner
Blooms: June–July
Deciduous vine

▶ **leaves up to 12 in. (30 cm) across**

Flowers: Insignificant. **Planting:** In spring. **Care:** High water requirement; apply slow-release fertilizer in spring and repeat at end of June; needs vertical supports for climbing; winter over outside with winter protection if necessary; pruning possible at end of June. **Propagating:** By cuttings taken in fall. **Design:** Dense growth offers outstanding privacy; however, grows very slowly at first. **Zone:** 4–8.

Silver Lace Vine, Silvervine Fleeceflower
Polygonum aubertii
Height: up to 35 ft (10 m); twiner
Deciduous vine

▶ **fast and vigorous grower**

Flowers: White, in long panicles. **Planting:** In spring. **Care:** High water requirement; fertilize every 2 weeks until August; sturdy support necessary; winter over outside with winter protection; tolerates and needs regular pruning. **Propagating:** By cuttings, taken shortly before flowering. **Design:** Clothes even very large surfaces with vigorous growth and development of side shoots and quickly offers privacy screening; very attractive with its lush flowering. **Zone:** 4–7.

EXPERT TIP
Caution: Can damage drainpipes!

Give vines that are to provide privacy the biggest container. It should hold 20–40 quarts (liters) of soil for the vine to produce enough leaves and flowers to cover a surface.

English Ivy

Hedera helix
Height: up to 20 ft or more (6 m); with aerial roots
Blooms: September
Evergreen vine

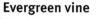

▶ **varieties with variegated leaves**

Flowers: Insignificant, yellow-green, only on older specimens; from these develop extremely poisonous black berries. **Planting:** In spring, train young plants on a support immediately. **Care:** Keep moderately damp; in April/May apply slow-release fertilizer; winter over outside, with winter protection; pruning possible at end of June. **Propagating:** By cuttings taken in fall. **Design:** Not only for climbing, also as trailing companion plants in boxes and hanging pots. **Zone:** 4–9.

Climbing Hydrangea

Hydrangea anomala ssp. *petiolaris*
Height: up to 16 ft (5 m); with aerial roots
Blooms: June–July
Deciduous vine

▶ **glowing yellow fall color**

Flowers: White, in corymbs 6–10 in. (15–25 cm) in size; appearing only after 2–4 years. **Planting:** In spring. **Care:** Keep damp; until August fertilize every 2 weeks; winter over outside, with winter protection as needed; prune very little. **Propagating:** By cuttings taken in summer. **Design:** Grows slowly at first, but really gets going after about the third year, then one of the most beautiful climbing plants. **Zone:** 4–7.

Winter Jasmine

Jasminum nudiflorum
Height: up to 15 ft (4.5 m); spreading climber
Blooms: January–March
Shrub with arching branches

▶ **valuable winter bloomer**

Flowers: Yellow, up to 2 in. (3 cm) Ø.
Planting: In spring or fall. **Care:** Keep moderately damp; apply slow-release fertilizer after blooming and open up every few years by pruning out canes that have finished blooming; fertilize every 2 weeks from start of new growth until August; winter over outside with winter protection as needed. **Propagating:** By cuttings taken in summer. **Design:** Supported on a trellis and tied up, an attractive vine with slightly arching growth habit. **Zone:** 5–11.

EXPERT TIP
Train up on a trellis; otherwise ivy can damage the wall surface.

EXPERT TIP
Climbs a wall without help, but a support is recommended.

EXPERT TIP
Green throughout winter, it doesn't lose its leaves until spring.

Hothouse Plants

When choosing hothouse plants for containers, don't just think of the summer location—suitable winter quarters must also be available.

Although the term "hothouse," or greenhouse, plants calls up visions of the luxurious conservatories of bygone days, there are many small woody plants that can be planted as specimens in large pots and maintained on a deck, balcony, or patio during the warm summer months. But because they come from warm climates and cannot withstand our harsh winters outside, they and their containers must be able to be moved to winter quarters.

Space-Grabbing Beauties

Most hothouse plants are native to the tropical or subtropical regions. This accounts for their need for warmth, for one thing, and for another, for their alluringly exotic charm, often with extraordinary flowers or growth forms. Usually expanding with time, many hothouse plants are more suitable for patios or courtyards than for the (small) deck or balcony. But you can enjoy the pleasure of exotic decoration there, too, if you choose slow-growing species and buy small

specimens. In addition, many plants can be propagated by cuttings, so a beauty that has grown too large can be replaced by its descendants. For eventually, with increasing (container) size, moving them inside becomes torture.

Vexing Issue: Overwintering

The majority of hothouse plants only do well in a bright, cool place over the winter—perhaps in a greenhouse or a large, light-filled stairwell. Fortunately, some species also tolerate dark overwintering. Very important: Never store these plants with a damp root ball! Old specimens of hemp palm, bay laurel, fig, oleander, and some other species can survive some frost and are better brought in late and taken out early, rather than staying too long in less-than-ideal winter quarters; when in doubt, protect them with row fabric, etc. Even with sun-loving hothouse plants it's advisable to place them in a lightly shaded spot at the beginning of the new fresh-air season, before they are subjected to the blazing sun.

Use of many hothouse plants provides a Mediterranean or tropical ambience on the deck, balcony, or patios in summer.

Sun-Worshiping Exotics

Paper Flower

Bougainvillea glabra
Height: up to 15 ft + (4.5 m); long shoots
Blooms: April–June
Deciduous climbing shrub

▶ **does well in front of bright south walls**

Flowers: Insignificant but with striking purple or white bracts. **Care:** Water copiously on hot days, fertilize weekly until August; grow up on posts fixed in pots or on trellises; cut back before bringing inside. **Propagating:** By softwood cuttings in spring. **Overwintering:** Bright at 46°–54° F (8°–12° C), withdraw water after leaf drop.
Design: Can be grown as a shrub, with supporting posts, as a vine, or as a standard.

Senna

Cassia corymbosa
Height: up to 8 ft (2.5 m); upright, branching
Blooms: July–October
Deciduous shrub

▶ **easy-care long bloomer**

Flowers: Yellow, very numerous in corymbs. **Care:** Keep well moistened, fertilize weekly until August.
Propagating: By softwood cuttings.
Overwintering: Tolerates light frost, don't move in too early; cut back and winter over dark at 36°–41° F (2°–5° C), keep slightly damp. **Design:** Effect as standard often somewhat scraggly, better to not prune off lower side branches.

Citrus Plants

Citrus species
Height: up to 5 ft + (1.5 m); bushy
Bloom: almost all year-round
Evergreen shrub

▶ **fragrant flowers**

Flowers: White or pale, pink; yellow or orange fruits. **Care:** Keep uniformly moist but never wet, fertilize weekly until August; support larger or fruit-bearing plants. **Overwintering:** Bring in early, keep bright at 39°–46° F (4°–8° C), water little, ventilate frequently; leaf drop in darker locations; don't place outside before the end of May, prune only every few years, as necessary. **Design:** Can be trained as a standard.

EXPERT TIP
A reliable and robust container variety is 'Sanderiana'.

EXPERT TIP
*Recommended is the Calamondin orange (x **Citrofortunella mitis**).*

**Reserve the sunniest, warmest places
for these plants. Unfortunately, during cool,
rainy summers, some will not bloom well.**

Cockspur Coral Tree, Cry-Baby Tree
Erythrina crista-galli
Height: up to 6 ft (1.8 m); bushy
Blooms: July–September
Deciduous shrub

▶ **really undemanding beauty**

Flowers: Strong coral red, in long clusters. **Care:** High water requirement, fertilize every 1–2 weeks until August. **Propagating:** By cuttings or seeds in spring. **Overwintering:** Before moving inside, cut back the year's growth to close to the trunk or to four eyes (to encourage more branching); keep dark at 43°–46° F (6°–8° C), withhold water; when new growth appears, move to a brighter, warmer place, water. **Design:** Especially effective in front of a white wall or near yellow summer flowers.

Common Olive
Olea europaea
Height: up to 7 ft (2 m); bushy to scraggly
Blooms: July–August
Evergreen shrub

▶ **Mediterranean decorative foliage**

Flowers: White, delicate, in clusters. **Care:** Keep evenly moist, fertilize every 2 weeks until August. Pruning possible at any time. **Propagating:** By softwood cuttings in summer. **Overwintering:** Old specimens tolerate some frost; keep at 36°–50° F (2°–10° C), light or dark; leaf drop when wintered over dark, then keep dry; move into protected spot outside as early as April. **Design:** Goes well with herbal plantings such as lavender and rosemary.

Canary Island Date
Phoenix canariensis
Height: up to 10 ft (3 m); spreading
Blooms: September
Evergreen tree

▶ **fast-growing, needs lots of space**

Flowers: Golden yellow, rare in container growing; ornamental because of leaf fans and growth form. **Care:** High water requirement, fertilize every 2–3 weeks until August; cut off dried fans. **Propagating:** By seed in spring. **Overwintering:** Light at 41°–50° F (5°–10° C), keep almost dry; after moving outside in May, place in shade at first, only move into full sun after 2 weeks. **Design:** Only looks and grows well in appropriately wide pots.

EXPERT TIP
With good care, blooms more and more lushly every year

EXPERT TIP
In pot culture, there are usually no olives to harvest.

The Most Beautiful Sun-Lovers

Sun-Loving Flowers

Name	Flower Color When Blooms	Overwintering
Flowering maple (*Abutilon* species)	red, orange, yellow all year	bright or dark 46°–54° F (8°–12° C)
Anisodontea (*Anisodontea capensis*)	dark pink May–September	bright 41°–50° F (5°–10° C)
Crimson bottlebrush (*Callistemon citrinus*)	red June–July	bright 41°–50° F (5°–10° C)
Canna (*Canna indica* hybrids)	red, yellow, white June–October	rhizome dark 41°–50° F (5°–10° C)
Bluebeard (*Caryopteris × clandonensis*)	blue August–September	light or dark 41°–50° F (5°–10° C)
Cestrum (*Cestrum elegans*)	red April–September	light 41°–50° F (5°–10° C)
Laudanum (*Cistus ladanifer*)	pink, red, white April–June	light 41°–50° F (5°–10° C)
Hebe (*Hebe × Andersonii* hybrids)	blue, red, while August–September	light 46°–50° F (8°–10° C)
Hibiscus (*Hibiscus rosasinensis*)	many color shades March–October	light 57°–61° F (14°–16° C)
Crape myrtle (*Lagerstroemia indica*)	rose, red, white August–October	dark 39°–46° F (4°–8° C)
Chilean jasmine (*Mandevilla laxa*)	white June–August	dark 39°–46° F (4°–8° C)
Lily (*Lilium* hybrids)	many color shades June–August	dark 32°–41° (0°–5° C)
Cape leadwort (*Plumbago auriculata*)	blue, white June–October	light or dark 39°–46° F (4°–8° C)
Pomegranate (*Punica granatum*)	red, yellow, white July–August	light or dark 36°–46° F (2°–8° C)

Lily of the Nile

Agapanthus hybrids, *A. praecox*
Height: up to 4 ft (1.2 m); broad clumps.
Blooms: July–August
Perennial, sometimes evergreen

▶ **avoid sogginess at all costs**

Flowers: Blue, violet, or white; trumpet-shaped, very numerous in umbels. **Care:** On hot days, water copiously, fertilize weekly until August. **Propagating:** By division in spring. **Overwintering:** Moderately bright at 39°–46° F (4°–8° C); keep evergreen forms slightly damp, deciduous ones dry (removing dead foliage); repot as seldom as possible. **Design:** Only looks right in wide pots, very beautiful also in halved barrels.

Argyranthemum

Argyranthemum frutescens
Height: 20–60 in. (0.5–1.5 m); broadly bushy
Blooms: all year-round
Subshrub

▶ **as bush or tree**

Flowers: White, pink, yellow; single and double varieties. **Care:** Water copiously on hot days, fertilize weekly until August; remove spent flowers and brown leaves. **Propagating:** By cuttings in spring; pinch back young plants frequently. **Overwintering:** As bright as possible at 39°–46° F (4°–8° C), keep slightly damp; if dark necessary, cut back by half first and keep almost dry. **Design:** Can be trained as a standard very nicely.

EXPERT TIP
Cutting back in spring promotes bushy growth.

During mild winters, the hothouse plant quarters should be ventilated for a short time every now and then; this prevents fungus diseases.

Lantana
Lantana camara hybrids
Height: 1–4 ft (0.3–1 m); bushy
Blooms: June–October
Deciduous shrub

▶ **constant butterfly attraction**

Flowers: Flowers in flat-topped heads, usually with ranges of color, for example from pink to red or from yellow to orange. **Care:** Keep uniformly moist, fertilize every 2 weeks until August; remove green berries when they appear. **Propagating:** From cuttings taken in spring. **Overwintering:** Bright, also dark after cutting back in fall, at 43°–50° F (6°–10° C), keep almost dry; cut branches back by half before moving inside or in spring. **Design:** Very beautiful grown as standard.

Oleander
Nerium oleander
Height: 5–8 ft (1.5–2.5 m); broadly bushy
Blooms: June–October
Evergreen shrub

▶ **some have intense fragrance**

Flowers: Pink, white, red, yellow; single or double in corymbs. **Care:** Water copiously, fill pot saucer with water, fertilize weekly until August; rain-protected location; inspect frequently for scale and aphids. **Propagating:** By cuttings taken in summer; they root well in water. **Overwintering:** Bright at 39°–46° F (4°–8° C), keeping almost dry; first cut off all branches that are bald or too long. **Design:** If possible group two or three different-colored specimens together.

Passionflower
Passiflora species
Height: 3–10 ft + (1–3 m); twining shoots
Blooms: June–September
Evergreen vine

▶ **extraordinarily distinctive flowers**

Flowers: White, violet, red, or yellow, with different-colored corona; up to 4 in. (10 cm) across. **Care:** Water copiously on hot days, fertilize weekly until August; support tendrils on bamboo poles in the pot or on trellises. **Propagating:** By cuttings from 1-year-old shoots in spring. **Overwintering:** Before moving inside cut back long vines, keep bright at 46°–54° F (8°–12° F) and almost dry; cut back ends of shoots in spring. **Design:** Deserves a privileged, wind-protected spot.

GOOD PARTNERS
Swan River daisy, lobelia, sweet alyssum as underplanting

EXPERT TIP
Caution: all plant parts are very poisonous!

EXPERT TIP
The passion fruits of P. edulis ripen in warm summers.

Sun-Loving Foliage Plants

Aeonium
Aeonium arboreum
Height: up to 3 ft (1 m); treelike form
Blooms: January–February
Evergreen succulent

▶ **tolerates even glaring sun**

Ornamentation: Thick, fleshy leaf rosettes, in 'Atropurpureum' brown to dark red; interesting growth habit; flowers only on older specimens. **Care:** Only water when the upper layer of soil is dried out; apply cactus fertilizer every 2 weeks until August. **Propagating:** By tip cuttings (entire rosettes with a piece of stem). **Overwintering:** Bright at 50°–54° F (10°–12° C), if necessary keep in a bright spot as a house plant; keep almost dry. **Design:** Very beautiful in slightly bulbous terra-cotta pots.

European Fan Palm
Chamaerops humilis
Height: 3–15 ft (1–4.5 m); shrublike
Blooms: not applicable
Evergreen tree

▶ **slow-growing**

Ornamentation: Large palm fans, over 20 in (50 cm) wide; dense growth. **Care:** Keep uniformly damp; fertilize weekly until August; a rain-protected place if possible. **Propagating:** From seed and division in spring. **Overwintering:** Only move inside when frost threatens; keep light or dark at 4°–50° F (5°–10° C), if necessary in a very bright place even somewhat warmer; water little. **Design:** With its dense, low-growing fans and its really compact growth habit, perhaps one of the most beautiful potted palms.

Common Fig
Ficus carica
Height: up to 8 ft (2.5 m); upright, branching
Blooms: spring, fall
Deciduous tree

▶ **very decorative foliage**

Ornamentation: Large, sturdy green, multilobed leaves, flowers inside small "jugs" from which fruits develop when conditions are favorable. **Care:** High water requirement, fertilize weekly until August. **Propagating:** By cuttings in spring. **Overwintering:** Tolerates some frost, take inside late; store bright, dark if necessary, at 36°–46° F (2°–8° C), water little; put outside as early as April, placing in shade at first. **Design:** One of the most beautiful foliage plants, with tropical charm.

GOOD PARTNERS
Place them next to bushy annuals like marigolds or heliotrope.

EXPERT TIP
The stems have thorns, use caution when moving!

Hothouse plants that achieve their effects solely through foliage and growth habit create calming accents between groupings of colorful flowers.

Bamboo
Phyllostachys species
Height: up to 8 ft (2.5 m); upright
Blooms: not applicable
Evergreen shrub

▶ **a breath of the Far East**

Ornamentation: Yellow or dark-colored, striped, or banded canes, delicate leaves. **Care:** Keep uniformly well dampened; wind-protected location; choose the widest possible containers for transplanting, divide larger specimens. **Propagating:** By division in spring. **Overwintering:** Keep bright at 41°–50° F (5°–10° C); water little; in spring cut out older canes. **Design:** An attractive privacy screen is provided by even two or three specimens.

Windmill Palm, Hemp Palm
Trachycarpus fortunei
Height: 5–13 ft (1.5–4 m); spreading
Blooms: not applicable
Evergreen tree

▶ **very slow-growing**

Ornamentation: Large, shining green leaf fans, over 20 in. (50 cm) long. **Care:** Keep moderately damp, fertilize every 3–4 weeks until August. **Propagating:** By seed. **Overwintering:** Tolerates frost, bring inside late; keep dark at 32°–46° F (0°–8° C) or in a bright place as a house plant; water little, and never in the heart; after moving outside in mid April, place in a shady spot at first. **Design:** Because of the slow growth you can also enjoy this robust palm in a small place for a long time.

Spanish Bayonet, Blue Yucca; Spineless Yucca
Yucca aloifolia; Y. elephantipes
Height: up to 8 ft (2.5 m); stiffly upright
Blooms: August–September
Evergreen tree

▶ **can be pruned without problems**

Ornamentation: Long, narrow leaves; white flowers, only on older specimens of *Y. elephantipes*. **Care:** Keep moderately damp, fertilize every 4 weeks until August, cut off brown leaves; specimens that have become too large will make new growth after being pruned back, as will the cut-off parts (cut into 12-in. [30-cm] lengths before potting up). **Propagating:** By tip or stem cuttings in summer, place pots in the shade. **Overwintering:** Bright at 41°–50° F (5°–10° C), keep almost dry. **Design:** Spanish yuccas provide a tropical or desert ambience.

EXPERT TIP
Very beautiful plants but in pot culture always somewhat tricky

EXPERT TIP
Place young specimens in part shade as a precaution.

EXPERT TIP
A beautiful variety with variegated leaves is 'Tricolor'.

Shade-Tolerant Flowers

Camellias

Camellia species
Height: up to 4 ft + (1.5 m); bushy
Blooms: January–April
Evergreen shrub

▶ **striking winter bloomer**

Flowers: White, pink, red, also bicolored; up to 5 in. (12 cm) Ø, single or double. **Care:** Keep moderately damp, give rhododendron (acidic) fertilizer weekly; with the appearance of buds (about the end of July) reduce watering, stop fertilizing; sprinkle frequently. **Propagation:** By cuttings taken in summer. **Overwintering:** Move inside to a bright place before frost, until the flowers open keep cool, while blooming at 59°–64° F (15°–18° C), water little. **Design:** Decorative foliage plant in summer. **Zone:** 7–9.

Angel's Trumpets

Datura and *Brugmansia* species
Height: up to 8 ft (2.5 m); shrub-, treelike
Blooms: July–September
Deciduous shrub/tree

▶ **intense fragrance in the evening**

Flowers: Pink, white, yellow, orange, blue; trumpet-shaped, up to 20 in. (50 cm) long. **Care:** Very high water and nutrient requirement, fertilize weekly until August, remove spent flowers; wind-protected situation. **Propagating:** By cuttings from spring to fall, also roots well in water. **Overwintering:** Bright or dark at 39°–54° F (4°–12° C); cut back before bringing indoors, especially in dark winter quarters; repot every spring, thinning if necessary. **Design:** White-flowering varieties look especially impressive. **Zone:** 10–11.

Hydrangea

Hydrangea macrophylla
Height: 20 in.–5 ft (0.5–1.5 m); broadly bushy
Blooms: May–July
Deciduous shrub

▶ **very lime-sensitive**

Flowers: Pink, red, blue, white; in large clusters up to 8 in. (20 cm). **Care:** Water copiously, give rhododendron (acidic) fertilizer every 2 weeks until August; regularly remove spent flowers. **Propagating:** By cuttings in early summer. **Overwintering:** Tolerates some frost; light or dark at 36°–46° F (2°–8° C), do not let root ball dry out; repot in spring (rhododendron soil), place in a brighter spot. **Design:** Goes very well with country-style planting schemes. **Zone:** 6–9.

EXPERT TIP
C. japonica *and* C. williamsii *hybrids offer a terrific range of varieties.*

EXPERT TIP
The fragrance can cause headaches in people who are sensitive to it.

Some gorgeous but quite poisonous summer bloomers thrive in sun to part shade, as do some rare beauties that flower in winter.

Iochroma
Iochroma cyaneum
Height: 3–5 ft (1–1.5 m); bushy
Blooms: July–August
Deciduous shrub

▶ **stems somewhat fragile**

Flowers: Violet, blue, red; small tubes in bunches. **Care:** Keep well dampened constantly, fertilize weekly until August; stake; wind-protected situation. **Propagating:** From tip cuttings in summer. **Overwintering:** Cut back before moving indoors, keep dark or light at 41°–54° F (5°–12° C), water little. **Design:** Makes a nice standard.

Blue Potato Bush
Solanum rantonnetii
Height: up to 7 ft (2 m); bushy
Blooms: July–October
Deciduous shrub

▶ **very lushly flowering**

Flowers: Violet with yellow eye, numerous. **Care:** High water requirement, fertilize weekly until August. **Propagating:** By softwood cuttings taken in summer. **Overwintering:** Cut back by half before moving inside, keep dark at 39°–50° F (4°–10° C), water very little; repot in March, move to a brighter, warmer spot. **Design:** Especially charming as small standard with yellow and red underplanting.

Laurustinus
Viburnum tinus
Height: 55–71 in. (1.4–1.8 m); bushy
Blooms: September–April
Evergreen shrub

▶ **flowers late and has ornamental leaves**

Flowers: White and numerous in flat racemes, slightly fragrant. **Care:** Keep uniformly damp, fertilize weekly until August. **Propagating:** By softwood cuttings in summer. **Overwintering:** Tolerates some frost, move inside late; keep bright at 32°–46° F (0°–8° C), water moderately. **Design:** Those who can keep the plant in a bright hallway or greenhouse will have the most flowers; during the summer a robust, attractive foliage plant. **Zone:** 7–9.

EXPERT TIP
The related species **S. jasminoides** *climbs and bears white flowers.*

Shade-Tolerant Foliage Plants

Century Plant, Maguey, American Aloe

Agave americana
Height: up to 6 ft (2 m); rosette
Blooms: not applicable
Evergreen succulent

▶ **becomes quite broad with age**

Ornamentation: Small, swordlike leaves, green or yellow- or white-edged, can attain more than 5 ft (1.5 m) in length. **Care:** Keep moderately damp; provide cactus fertilizer once in spring. **Propagating:** By daughter plants (offsets). **Overwintering:** Before moving inside and outside, put corks on the dangerously sharp tips; bright at 48° F (5° C), keep almost dry. **Design:** Out of the ordinary, but interesting: yellow-edged varieties look lovely in blue tubs.

Japanese Aucuba, Japanese Laurel

Aucuba japonica
Height: up to 8 ft (2.5 m); broadly bushy
Blooms: March–April
Evergreen shrub

▶ **sturdy decoration for shade**

Ornamentation: Densely covered with attractive foliage, usually yellow flecked or dotted; flowers insignificant; sometimes glowing red (poisonous) berries. **Care:** Keep well dampened; fertilize every 4 weeks until August; rain-protected location if possible. **Propagating:** By softwood cuttings in spring and summer. **Overwintering:** Tolerates some frost, bring inside late; keep in a bright and in a just barely frost-free spot; water little; move out again in April. **Design:** One of the most attractive foliage plants. **Zone:** 7–11.

Sago Palm, Japanese Sago Palm, Japanese Fern Palm

Cycas revoluta
Height: up to 8 ft + (2.5 m); nestlike
Blooms: not applicable
Evergreen shrub

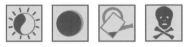

▶ **grows extraordinarily slowly**

Ornamentation: Long, slightly arching, leathery, finely pinnated fans, dark green. **Care:** Water only when the upper surface of the soil has dried out; fertilize every 4 weeks until August with weakened solution; protect from rain as well as possible. **Overwintering:** Bright at 54°–59° F (12°–15° C); keep almost dry. **Design:** Even on some shady decks there is almost always a space for a Sago palm, which are usually available as dainty young plants.

EXPERT TIP
Caution: risk of injury from pointed ends and thorny leaf edges!

EXPERT TIP
When wintered over too warm, frequently gets leaf spot disease

The choice of hothouse plants for really shady spots is small, but good. Here the strongly expressive foliage plants are trumps.

Abyssinian Banana
Ensete ventricosum
Height: up to 10 ft + (3 m); palmlike
Blooms: not applicable
Long-lived large shrub

▶ **fast-growing and spreading**

Ornamentation: Very large, decorative leaves. **Care:** High water requirement; fertilize weekly until August; wind-protected location. **Propagating:** By seed from January to April. **Overwintering:** Cut back to the leaves at the heart before moving indoors; situate in light at 50° F (10° C); water little, and never into the "heart." **Design:** Specimens are very effective but need a great deal of space; on the patio, the cockspur coral tree, angel's trumpets, or palms are suitable neighbors.

Sweet Bay
Lauris nobilis
Height: up to 7 ft + (2 m); upright, bushy
Blooms: April–May
Evergreen shrub

▶ **grows very slowly**

Ornamentation: Dense, dark green, glossy foliage; flowers (insignificant) only on unpruned plants. **Care:** Keep uniformly damp; fertilize weekly until August. **Propagating:** By cuttings, growing is very slow. **Overwintering:** Bring in late, tolerates some frost; bright, dark if necessary, keep at 32°–43° F (0°–6° C), water little; prune, if desired, in March; can be placed outside after the middle of April. **Design:** Is often trained as a pyramid or a small tree with a balled crown. **Zone:** 8–11.

New Zealand Flax
Phormium tenax
Height: up to 5 ft + (1.5 m); nestlike
Blooms: August–September
Evergreen shrub

▶ **very undemanding plant**

Ornamentation: Long, narrow, sword-shaped leaves, which are green, reddish, or yellow- or white-striped, depending on the variety; red flower panicles only on older specimens. **Care:** In sunny spots, water copiously, otherwise moderately, fertilize weekly until August. **Propagating:** By division in spring. **Overwintering:** Bring inside as soon as frost threatens; keep light or dark at 39°–50° F (4°–10° C), water little; remove dried leaves from time to time. **Design:** Can be underplanted in large containers with small annuals or ivy.

EXPERT TIP
Harvest leaves for the kitchen as needed.

Herbs, Vegetables, Fruit

Fresh-picked to the table — many herbs, vegetables, and fruits can be successfully and attractively grown in pots on decks, balconies, and patios.

You won't be able to fill a root cellar with the harvest from containers and boxes. But still, the enjoyment of fresh, home-grown produce again and again is such a special experience that soon you will no longer want to be without it.

Fruit Growing Is a Science in Itself
Instructions on the culture of fruit very quickly fill up entire books. In particular, the raising (training) of young trees and their further pruning requires some detailed knowledge, especially as there are also differences among the various fruit varieties and tree forms. To start with, expert advice at the place of purchase about these matters is very useful; the special scientific literature is helpful if you want to pursue the interest (see Resources on page 152). These points are of primary importance:

▶ Choose varieties or shapes that are not constituted to be very vigorous growers.

▶ It's best to buy container plants in spring that have already been raised in pots.

▶ Besides the species described on pages 118–119, there are still many others to consider, such as dwarf peaches or nectarines, which always look very pretty in garden catalogs. However, these plants need a particularly warm, protected situation, especially when they are in bloom and in winter.

Buying Plants and Pot Size
Growing plants is fun — when it's successful. With varieties requiring warmth, like tomatoes, peppers, or cucumbers, however, there is a definite advantage to buying well-developed young plants so that they will also begin to fruit earlier.

Tomatoes, etc., but above all, fruit trees, need the largest pots possible. For fruiting shrubs and small trees you should start with a container of not less than 8 qts (8 L) in volume; over the years 20–40-quart (20–40-L) pots become necessary. It is imperative that you consider the weight of such containers and check the weight tolerance of your deck first.

Good to look at and to eat — for many people, tomatoes, berries, and apples are the most beautiful ornaments to a deck.

Annual Herbs

Dill
Anethum graveolens
Height: 20–36 in. (50–90 cm); upright
Blooms: July–August
Annual herb

▶ **handsome yellow umbels**

Growing: Broadcast sow from April to July in deep boxes or pots, slightly thin seedlings when they are sprouting densely; also use as companion plants to other herbs or vegetables. **Care:** Keep only slightly damp; fertilizing unnecessary. **Harvest:** Young leaves possible all summer long; seed harvest hardly pays in pot culture.

Chervil
Anthriscus cerefolium
Height: 12–24 in. (30–60 cm); bushy
Blooms: June–August
Annual herb

▶ **slightly lime-sensitive**

Growing: Sow directly in boxes, pots, or saucer planters from the beginning of April/May, thin to 4–6 in. (10–15 cm) apart; successive sowings every 2–3 weeks until June. **Care:** Part-shady location and constantly moist soil retards the (undesirable) flowers in summer; during the growing period fertilize lightly once. **Harvest:** Constantly harvest fresh young leaves; the anise-like flavor is only intense before flowers appear and rounds out salads, cottage cheese, sauces, and soups.

Borage
Borago officinalis
Height: 24–32 in. (60–80 cm); bushy
Blooms: June–August
Annual herb

▶ **very attractive blue flowers**

Growing: Sow April to June in boxes or pots at least 8 in. (20 cm) deep, thin seedlings to 10–12 in. (25–30 cm) apart. **Care:** Water copiously on sunny days, fertilize lightly every 4 weeks; remove spent flowers. **Harvest:** Pick young leaves all summer long; the flowers are also edible and can be used to decorate food and drinks.

EXPERT TIP
Dill also loosens up flower bouquets.

EXPERT TIP
Keeps aphids away, therefore a good partner for lettuce

EXPERT TIP
Can be combined beautifully with calendulas in mixed boxes

Taking up only the smallest amount of space, annual herbs supply the kitchen's fresh seasoning needs right into the fall.

Garden Cress
Lepidium sativum
Height: 8–12 in. (20–30 cm); bushy
Blooms: July–August
Annual herb

▶ **fast-growing and undemanding**

Growing: Successive sowings every 2 weeks from March to September, directly in boxes or saucer planters; broadcast seeds, press in gently and cover lightly with soil. **Care:** Keep evenly moist, do not fertilize; with enough warmth, thrives even in shade. **Harvest:** Usually you can cut off the young shoots directly at the soil surface as early as 10 days after sowing, as soon as they are about 2½ in. (6 cm) high.

Basil
Ocimum basilicum
Height: 8–24 in. (20–60 cm); bushy
Blooms: July–September
Annual herb

▶ **full sun if possible**

Growing: Sow in April/May, light-germinator, do not cover; prick out seedlings; after last frost plant in pots or deck boxes, 10 in. (25 cm) apart. **Care:** Before cool May nights, cover with floating row cover; keep evenly damp, fertilize every 4 weeks; put in wind- and rain-protected spot. **Harvest:** Leaves and young shoots all summer long; harvest growing tips first, then plants will grow bushier; more flavorful before flowers appear; pinch off flowers to prolong harvest.

Summer Savory
Satureja hortensis
Height: 12–16 in. (30–40 cm); bushy
Blooms: July–October
Annual herb

▶ **needs warmth**

Growing: To start ahead of time, sow in April (light-germinator); plant after the last frost in pots or boxes or sow directly in boxes in mid May; thin to 10 in. (25 cm) apart; make successive sowings until the beginning of June. **Care:** Protect with a floating row cover from cool May nights; keep evenly moist, fertilize lightly once during the growing period; wind-protected location. **Harvest:** Young shoots all summer long; most flavorful shortly before and during flowering; cut off flowering shoots for drying.

EXPERT TIP
Combines well with other herbs and vegetables as a "ground cover"

EXPERT TIP
Variegated, also colored-leaved variety: 'Purple Ruffles'

EXPERT TIP
Good seasoning for bean, potato, and meat dishes as well as soups

Biennial and Perennial Herbs

Chives
Allium schoenoprasum
Height: 8–18 in. (20–45 cm); clumps
Blooms: June–August
Perennial

▶ **prettily arranged flowers**

Growing: Sow in March or April, then plant seedlings in bunches (10–20 plantlets) in pots or boxes; after April, put outside, in light shade if possible.
Care: Keep evenly well moistened, fertilize every 2 weeks until August; if more leaf development is desired, pinch off the flowers; winter over bright and cool, keep almost dry. **Harvest:** Cut off tubular leaves ³/₄ in. (2 cm) above the soil surface about 6 weeks after sowing, then just let new growth develop again; harvest until fall. **Zone:** 3–11.

Oregano
Origanum vulgare
Height: 8–24 in. (20–60 cm); broadly bushy
Blooms: July–September
Perennial

▶ **give as much sun as possible**

Growing: Sow in March or April, light-germinator; put one to two plants in a wide pot or saucer planter; after the beginning of May place outside, possibly with slight protection at night.
Care: Keep evenly slightly moist, no fertilizer; cut back in October and provide with winter protection or winter over inside frost free and moderately bright. **Harvest:** Pick leaves and young growing tips for use fresh from the end of May until fall. **Zone:** 3–9.

Parsley
Petroselinum crispum ssp. *crispum*
Height: 8–18 in. (20–45 cm); bushy
Blooms: June–July (2nd year)
Biennial herb

▶ **curly- and smooth-leaved varieties**

Growing: Sow from middle of March to June directly in final container (germination may take up to 3 weeks); separate the small plants to 4 in. (10 cm) apart; place outside starting in April/early May, protect from frosty nights with floating row cover or the like. **Care:** Keep evenly moist, fertilize lightly every 2 weeks; winter over outside with protection or in a light, frost-free spot inside. **Harvest:** Eight to 10 weeks after sowing, with March sowing, starting in June; keep harvesting leaves until just before flowers appear in the second year.

EXPERT TIP
Divide and replant in spring or fall every 2–3 years.

EXPERT TIP
The flavor is most intense during flowering.

GOOD PARTNERS
Tomatoes, radishes—do not combine with lettuce

Besides parsley and chives there are many Mediterranean herbs to enrich the cuisine and the deck with their intense flavor, aromatic fragrance, and pretty flowers.

Rosemary
Rosmarinus officinalis
Height: 2–3 ft (60–90 cm); broadly bushy
Blooms: March–April
Evergreen shrub

▶ **distinctive aromatic fragrance**

Growing: Tedious, better to buy young plants and put them alone in large pots; propagation possible from cuttings in August. **Care:** Keep uniformly slightly damp, fertilize every 8 weeks until August; winter over bright at 36°–46° F (2°–8° C), don't put outside until mid May; repot old plants only rarely. **Harvest:** Pick leaves and growth tips constantly from spring to fall, being careful not to pick too much at once; harvest leaves for drying in summer. **Zone:** 7–11.

Sage
Salvia officinalis
Height: 12–20 in. (30–50 cm); broadly bushy
Blooms: June–August
Long-lived plant

▶ **ornamental blue-violet flowers**

Growing: Sow outdoors from April to May, later plant the young plants 12 in. (30 cm) apart or one to two per pot; propagation by cutting possible in summer. **Care:** Water little, fertilize every 8 weeks until August; winter over outside with protection or inside bright and frost-free; in spring cut back by a good half. **Harvest:** Pick young, delicate leaves from May to October; for drying, cut stems just before flowers appear. **Zone:** 4–9.

Thyme
Thymus vulgaris
Height: 8–16 in. (20–40 cm); bushy
Blooms: June–September
Evergreen

▶ **intense aroma**

Growing: Difficult, better to buy young plants, plant in May, 8 in. (20 cm) apart; with older plants, propagation possible by cuttings in summer and division in fall. **Care:** Keep slightly moist, winter over indoors, bright, cool, and almost dry; cut back in spring, then fertilize lightly. **Harvest:** Cut young leaves and growth tips from spring to fall; most aromatic just before blooming. **Zone:** 5–9.

EXPERT TIP
Attractive container plants with blue flowers and blue-green leaves

EXPERT TIP
Variety 'Tricolor' with yellow-white-reddish patterned leaves

EXPERT TIP
With its little pink or violet flowers, also a pretty ornamental plant

Vegetables in Tubs and Boxes

Vegetables for Pots and Boxes

Name Height in Inches (cm)	Sowing	When to Plant Planting Distance
Artichokes 3–4 ft (90–120 cm)	from March, start indoors	late spring plant singly
Arugula 12–24 in. (30–60 cm)	from April–August, direct sow	early to mid spring broadcast sow
Beans, bush 16–24 in. (40–60 cm)	mid April, start indoors	late spring/early summer 12–16 in. (30–40 cm)
Beans, pole 5–8 ft (1.5–2.5 m) (twining)	end April, start indoors	late spring/early summer 2–4 plants in large pot
Beans, scarlet runner up to 10 ft (3 m+) (twining)	end April, start indoors	late spring/early summer 2–4 plants in large pot
Broccoli 2–3 ft (60–90 cm)	in March, start indoors	after last frost 14–16 in. (35–40 cm)
Cucumbers 20–48 in.+ (50–120 cm+) (creeping/vining)	in April, start indoors	after last frost plant singly
Eggplant 20–36 in. (50–90 cm)	mid March, start indoors	after last frost plant singly
Feldsalat 2–6 in. (5–15 cm)	mid-August–September, direct sow	early spring broadcast sow
Kohlrabi 12–16 in. (30–40 cm)	in March, start indoors	mid spring 10–12 in. (25–30 cm)
Melons up to 6 ft+ (2 m+) (creeping/vining)	in April, start indoors	after last frost plant singly
Peas, sugar snap 2–6 ft ($\frac{1}{2}$–2 m) (creeping/vining)	mid April–May, direct sow	early spring 1$\frac{1}{2}$–2 in. (4–5 cm)
Peppers 12–30 in. (30–75 cm)	in March, start indoors	after last frost plant singly
Pumpkin/Squash up to 6 ft+ (2 m+) (creeping/vining)	from end of April, start indoors	after last frost plant singly
Spinach 4–12 in. (10–20 cm)	from February–May, direct sow	early spring broadcast sow
Spinach, New Zealand 8–12 in. (20–30 cm)	end of April, start indoors	late spring/early summer plant singly

Chard
Beta vulgaris ssp. *vulgaris*
Height: 18–28 in. (45–70 cm); upright
Harvest: July–September
Leaf vegetable

▶ **as leaf or stem chard**

Growing: Sow in large tubs or boxes from end of April to June; thin young plants to 10 in. (25 cm) apart. **Care:** Always keep well moistened, fertilize every 4 weeks. **Harvest:** Constantly, always harvest outer leaves; prepare leaf chard varieties like spinach, stem chard like asparagus; with some varieties like 'Lucullus', stems and leaves can be used.

Zucchini
Concurbita pepo
Height: 20–24 in. (50–60 cm); spreading
Harvest: July–September
Fruiting vegetable

▶ **also yellow-fruited varieties**

Growing: Sow two seeds per pot at end of April, remove weaker plants after sprouting; plant in wide pots, place outside after the last frost. **Care:** Always keep well watered, don't water into flowers, fertilize weekly. **Harvest:** Pick fruit constantly, don't let grow too large (8 in. [20 cm] long maximum).

EXPERT TIP
An attractive variety with red, yellow, pink, and gold stems is 'Bright Lights'.

EXPERT TIP
As a rule, two plants are more than enough.

**Special deck varieties of many
vegetables are available, and they produce excellent
harvests even in pots, boxes, and tubs.**

Leaf and Head Lettuce

Lactuca sativa var. *crispa*
Height: 8–12 in. (20–30 cm); rosette
Harvest: From May onward
Annual salad plant

▶ **sow in several batches**

Growing: From March; sow head lettuce in two rows directly in boxes,
start leaf lettuce inside and plant at
least 8–10 in. (20–25 cm) apart; outdoors, from April, with protection; successive sowings for head lettuce until
April, leaf lettuce until July. **Care:** Keep
uniformly moist, fertilize again lightly
after each cutting. **Harvest:** For head
lettuce harvest the entire plant, for
leaf lettuce keep plucking the lowest
leaves.

Tomatoes, Cherry Tomatoes

Lycopersicon lycopersicum
Height: 10–60 in. (25–150 cm);
upright/bushy
Harvest: July–October
Fruiting vegetable

▶ **all green parts are poisonous**

Growing: Sow from March at 68° F
(20° C); prick out to one per 4-in.
(10-cm) pot, place in a bright situation
at 64° F (18° C); plant in large containers or boxes, at least 10 in. (25 cm)
apart; move outdoors after last frost.
Care: Stake high-growing varieties; always keep well watered, fertilize
weekly; plant seedlings at least 2 in.
deeper in the soil than they were in
their containers to help anchor plants
and stimulate root development.
Harvest: Pick fruits when they are
fully ripened.

Radish

Raphanus sativus var. *sativus*
Height: 4–6 in. (10–15 cm); compact
Harvest: May–September
Root vegetable

▶ **must be sown in loose soil**

Growing: Sow directly in boxes or
saucer planters from end of March to
August, with successive sowings every
few weeks; different varieties for
spring and summer sowing (read the
information on the seed packets);
after sprouting, thin the developed
seedlings to 2½–3 in. (6–8 cm) apart.
Care: Keep uniformly moist, fertilizing
not necessary. **Harvest:** About 6
weeks after sowing in spring, in summer 3–4 weeks after sowing; don't
wait too long or the radishes become
"furry"; always take the biggest
radishes first.

EXPERT TIP
*Good deck plants are bush,
cherry, and trailing tomatoes.*

GOOD PARTNERS
Tomatoes, lettuce, chard, parsley

Fruit for Balconies and Patios

Kiwi
Actinidia chinensis
Height: up to 10 ft (3 m); climbing
Harvest: End October/November
Twining vine

▶ **wind-sheltered place**

Growing: With dioecious varieties, male and female plants necessary for development of fruit; train on a trellis. **Care:** Keep evenly well moistened, apply slow-release fertilizer in spring, fertilize again in June and at beginning of August; protect well if wintered over outside; training pruning and rejuvenation pruning necessary every few years. **Varieties:** Dioecious: 'Hayward', 'Weiki' (very frost-hardy); monoecious (self-fertilizing): 'Jenny', 'Oriental Delight'. **Zone:** 5–9.

Strawberries
Fragaria vesca
Height: 12 in. (30 cm); various forms
Harvest: June–September/October
Perennial

▶ **replant every 2–3 years**

Growing: In boxes, pots, in large tubs as underplanting of shrubs; also as vining strawberries with long shoots and hanging strawberries for baskets; simple propagation from runners. **Care:** Keep uniformly moist, apply slow-release fertilizer in spring; remove withered leaves in fall and spring; winter over outdoors with protection. **Varieties:** Numerous small-fruited (everbearing) and large-fruited varieties, also climbing forms. **Zone:** 4–8.

Apple
Malus domestica
Height: 3–7 ft (1–2 m); different forms
Harvest: August–October
Tree

▶ **choose slow-growing forms**

Growing: Two to three different varieties that bloom at the same time, necessary to guarantee fruiting; in planting, the thickened graft union must be above the soil surface. **Care:** Keep uniformly moist, apply slow-release fertilizer in spring, fertilize again in June as needed; winter over outdoors with protection; regular training and containing pruning necessary; repot every few years. **Varieties:** "Ballerina" varieties (bred without side branches) such as 'Waltz', 'Polka'; otherwise almost all varieties grafted to dwarfing stock. **Zone:** 3–8 (varies by cultivar).

EXPERT TIP
Thrives better in bright west or east locations than in front of a blazing south wall

EXPERT TIP
Water well in August/September (time of new flower development).

EXPERT TIP
Suitable tree forms are Collonades, or columnar dwarf trees.

Late frosts during the flowering season in spring are especially critical for tree and shrub fruits; cover them or bring them inside when frost threatens.

Plum, Damson
Prunus domestica
Height: 5–8 ft (1.5–2.5 m); broad crown
Harvest: August–October
Tree

▶ **robust fruit species**

Growing: Preferably, plant self-fertilizing varieties (no pollinating variety necessary) on dwarfing understock (with graft union above the soil surface). **Care:** Keep evenly well moistened, in spring apply slow-release fertilizer, fertilize again every 8 weeks until August; support fruit-bearing limbs; winter over with protection; after training pruning, only regular thinning is necessary; repot every few years. **Varieties:** 'Stark Blue Ribbon', 'Fellemberg', 'Stanley'. **Zone:** 4–9.

Pear
Pyrus communis
Height: 5–7 ft (1.5–2 m); various forms
Harvest: End August–October
Tree

▶ **especially needs warmth**

Growing: Two to three different varieties necessary for fertilization; plant so that the graft union is above soil surface. **Care:** Keep evenly moist, in spring apply slow-release fertilizer, refertilize in June if necessary; support fruit-bearing branches; winter over outside with protection; regular pruning necessary for growth training and good health; repot every few years.
Varieties: 'Moonglow', 'Kieffer', 'Seckel', 'Beuppe D'Anjou'. **Zone:** 4–9.

Currant
Ribes rubrum, R. nigrum
Height: 3–5 ft (1–1.5 m); broadly bushy
Harvest: July–August
Shrub

▶ **very attractive as a standard**

Growing: Self-fertilizing (no pollinating varieties necessary); can be planted as a shrub, standard, or small standard, preferably in slightly acid soil. **Care:** Keep uniformly well moistened, provide slow-release fertilizer in spring, then fertilize every 8 weeks until August; stake tall standard; winter over outside with protection; after harvest or in winter, prune out older canes. **Varieties:** 'Red Lake' (red), 'Wilder' (red), 'Prince Consort' (black). **Zone:** 3–6.

EXPERT TIP
The same species also includes Japanese plums and 'Green Gage' plums.

EXPERT TIP
Ask for varieties with good fireblight resistance.

Designing Decks

and Patios

Designing Decks and Patios

Designing with Plants and Containers
Pages 122–131

Plant Combinations
Pages 132–149

Designing with

Plants and Containers

Most important design ground rule: Whatever you like is allowed. You should be completely comfortable in your own individually designed environment.

Have lots of colored flowers, add in a few decorative pots—what's left to design? So you might wonder when you have to get along with 65 ft² (6 m²) of "deck." But it's with just such narrowly bounded areas that you can do a great deal by skillful arrangement. Thus, for instance, a place for some fruit or vegetables for nibbling can be integrated into the design economically and pleasingly. Flowering standards are terrific eye-catchers, while being much less space-hogging than bushy, spreading potted shrubs. And even that enchanting element, the water garden, can have great effect in the form of a miniature version.

Rules and Experiments

There are innumerable interesting possibilities for beautifying decks or patios, so that sometimes one has to suffer the torture of making choices. Keep in mind:
▶ Most of all, the limiting factors are—besides the area available—all the light conditions on the decks and patios; these establish the framework for the planting.
▶ Various "rules," such as those for putting colors or shapes together, are very helpful as reference points but are not immutable laws.
▶ Feel free to experiment once in a while—all kinds of excitement and beauty can result.
▶ Unlike a garden, decks and patios can be recreated each year—even monthly, if necessary—and offer the opportunity to keep trying out something new.

Boxes, Hanging Pots, Tubs, Pots

It's not only the plants in different colors and forms that shape the appearance of a deck or a patio—the different plant containers play a role in the design as well. They can tie the various plant groups together, provide color contrast, or offer additional decoration. And more different decorative elements can be added according to desire and mood.

Great effect with a small space: well-coordinated planting with decorative accents.

Creating Harmony, Placing Accents

The multitude of possible arrangements, available plants, and accessories available is gratifying. But this can easily lead to overloading, to "overstuffing" the limited planting or standing area—and in the end you may not be so happy with the result, despite the colorful profusion of flowers.

Varied Plant Levels

Creating a harmonious total picture becomes easier if you first clarify the basic planting options, their functions, and plant levels:

▶ Deck boxes serve the middle, medium-high level, on landings, on the windowsill, or on the low patio walls; in the foreground of a deck or balcony they are almost "a must." Planted with combinations of long-lasting summer flowers, possibly augmented by spring or fall flowers, they continuously define the total picture. When the railings on an open deck or balcony also run around the short sides, tall pot plants or vines can replace the boxes with a privacy fence there.

▶ One to two large eye-catchers are entirely enough to start with. These can be standards or small fruit trees, for instance, or an attractive flowering shrub or a water garden. These decorative elements also work their effects at middle height, but they require plenty of surface area; bear in mind that the necessary space for the plants can quickly use up more than 10 ft² (1 m²) of sitting or traffic area.

▶ If there is still room on the floor surface, a tiny group of dishes or smaller pots, preferably placed in the corners, is very pretty. Here also an effective gradation of heights can be created through use of flower stands or shelves.

▶ Leaving the floor, there is more room on the "upper floors," and if there is no ceiling, you can perhaps manage with side wall brackets. An attractively planted hanging pot or a hanging basket is often enough to provide an airy accent.

▶ There is still the vertical plane, which can be furnished with climbing plants, either with pots fastened to a trellis or with the help of a plant stand.

Less Is Often More

At first—especially on a small deck—use only three or four of the suggested plant choices.

The combination of different planting levels provides for a pleasing structure even with a small planting, and you will soon get a sense for anything still missing and what it might be.

Finally, there are two more important aspects of plant use:

▶ Particularly ornamental plants also require visual space. An attractive hothouse plant is at its most effective against a quiet background, with some distance between it and colorful boxes of annuals.

▶ Use repetition and symmetry: If, for example, you limit yourself to only two plant combinations that alternate in the deck boxes lined up in a row, a more defined total picture results.

Symmetry is also very effective, such as having matching globes of boxwood or argyranthemums standing to the right and left of a door.

Various Decorating Possibilities
Pinwheels, clay suns or moons, reflecting balls, garden gnomes—if it's what you like, it works.

Impressive hothouse plants like these angel's trumpets show to best advantage when grown as single specimens.

The Inanimate Elements

It's not just the plantings that determine the total design picture:

▶ Handsome plant containers can be artfully positioned to serve as striking style elements. Whether they be terra-cotta or rustic wooden tubs, or dark, "natural" stoneware or brightly glazed—this depends entirely on personal taste.

▶ Also matters of taste are the countless decorative elements for decks and patios available commercially. Colorful weathervanes, terra-cotta bears, rose balls—why not, if you like them?

▶ Also included in the area of personal preference is the choice of colorful chairs, tables, and table covers. Nevertheless, you should not underestimate how much colored furniture and other objects can alter and even encroach on the effect of a planting. Certainly from a design point of view, neutral furniture in white or made of light wood is the most compatible solution.

The Small Feel-Good Elements

Intriguing variety, total harmony, fabulous arrangements—it's easy to go into raptures at the sight of a beautiful deck. So it seems almost heretical to bring up the practical aspects of everyday deck life. The deck isn't just there to look at, though; in the summer it functions primarily as a "green living room." And a few apparently very banal trifles must be right so people really feel good there. For example: Is there enough space left for comfortable sitting? Are all the plants easily accessible for watering and for other maintenance jobs? Can they be moved without a gigantic effort if it ever becomes necessary? Can you also, if necessary, carry a tray loaded with food or drinks to the deck table without having to go through an acrobatic act? Or put your feet up if you want to?

Those who take such practical "trivialities" into consideration in the design will get the most pleasure out of their deck or patio in the long run.

EXPERT TIP
Make sure deck furniture is of weatherproof materials.

CROSS-REFERENCE
Plant Combinations pages 132–148

Training and Underplanting Small Standards

Information in Brief

Tools, Material

Pruning shears
Garden string or raffia
Wooden or bamboo stake
(about 5 ft [1.5 m] long)

Time Needed

Training a standard:
2–3 years
Developing a crown:
about 2 years

Plants Suitable for Standards

Flowering maple (*Abutilon* species)
Argyranthemum (*Argyranthemum frutescens*)
Bougainvillea (*Bougainvillea glabra*)
Calamondin (*Citrus x Citrofortunella*)
Fuchsia (*Fuchsia* hybrids)
Iochroma (*Iochroma cyaneum*)
Lantana (*Lantana camara* hybrids)
Oleander (*Nerium oleander*)
Cape plumbago (*Plumbago auriculata*)
Blue potato bush (*Solanum rantonnetii*)

Removing Side Shoots, Tying

Select a sturdy young plant with a clearly defined main stem that is as nearly straight as possible. Cut off any side shoots cleanly and bind the plant firmly to a supporting stake, using loose figure-eight knots.

Cutting Back

At first fertilize rather sparingly with a low-nitrogen fertilizer and only until the beginning of August so that the stem develops good woodiness. The first steps toward creating a beautiful crown come when the desired height (about 48 in. [1.2 m]) is reached: As soon as some pairs of leaves and side shoots have developed in the upper region, cut off the tips to promote branching.

The formation of standards requires patience and doesn't always succeed on the first try. But the result is worth all the effort.

Pinching Off Side Shoots

Finally the side shoots are pinched off, back to the second or third pair of leaves. Thus a compact crown is gradually developed. Keep cutting back the tips, also any new side shoots that grow from the stem. If it hasn't been done already, the trunk should now also be tied to the stake with figure eight knots directly below the crown. If repotting becomes necessary, you must of course work very carefully and immediately stabilize the stem again.

Underplanting—Example 1

Patience is rewarded when—as shown here—a lantana turns into a flowering centerpiece. When the containers are large enough, bellflowers (*Campanula carpatica, C. poscharskyana*) make a gorgeous underplanting. Start in April/May and carefully dig planting holes close to the edge of the pot and, depending on the size of the container, put in 3–5 bellflowers. Take out the spent bellflowers in September and winter them over in separate pots.

Underplanting—Example 2

Here three red hanging verbenas (*Verbena* × hybrida), four annual black-eyed Susans (*Rudbeckia hirta*), and two Swedish ivies (*Plectranthus*) provide an opulent base for the blue-flowering blue potato bush (*Solanum rantonnetii*). Don't plant such rampant companions until June, when the standard has become well developed after being moved outside in mid to late May and can withstand the competition. This combination needs plenty of water and fertilizer. The blue potato bush often develops thin, whiplike shoots that should be regularly shortened in summer.

EXPERT TIP
Geraniums (Pelargoniums) can also be trained as standards.

CROSS-REFERENCE
Hothouse Plants pages 98–109

Water Garden Focal Point

Information in Brief

Plants for Depths of 8–20 in. (20–50 cm)

Pickerel weed *(Pontederia cordata)*
Water lilies *(Nymphaea* 'Uber Gold', 'Laydekeri Lilacea', 'Laydekeri Purpurea')
Yellow floating-heart *(Nymphoides peltata)*
Pond bulrush *(Scirpus lacustris* 'Albescens')

Plants for Depths of 4–12 in. (10–30 cm)

Sweet flag *(Acorus calamus)*
Mad-dog weed *(Alisma plantago-aquatica)*
Water gladiolus *(Butomus umbellatus)*
Dwarf water lilies *(Nymphaea pygmaea* varieties)

Marsh Plants

Cowslip *(Caltha palustris)*
Moneywort *(Lysimachia nummularia)*
Purple loosestrife *(Lythrum salicaria)*
Swamp forget-me-not *(Myosotis palustris)*

Small Water Lily Paradise
The element of water can be introduced in this charming way on even a small deck. Two water lilies (yellow-orange 'Indiana', dwarf water lily 'Rubra') and an arrowhead represent the pond plant world, a floating stone and floating candles enhance the decorative arrangement. Terra-cotta pots that serve as pond containers must be glazed inside. Such small ponds can be transported entire into suitable winter quarters (bright, frost-free, max. 41° F [5° C]).

Small Marsh Garden in Part Shade
Yellow flags *(Iris pseudacorus)* tolerate depths up to 12 in. (30 cm), but they also thrive in damp soil (single-purpose soil with additions of compost and loam). Here two are planted in combination with perennial monkey flowers *(Mimulus luteus)*, which also like moisture. The planting can take a half day of shade and can be wintered over outside with light protection. Beautiful companions in neighboring pots: swamp forget-me-nots and ragged robin *(Lychnis flos-cuculi)*

Frogs only appear on the deck or patio as stone ornaments. But birds, and also the occasional dragonfly, gladly drop in on a water garden once in a while.

A Pretty Combo Water Garden

The combination of several pots offers advantages: The single pots can be carried much more easily than one large pot, plant combinations can be rearranged at will or moved to a more favorable location, and plants with differing requirements can be planted separately and yet create their effect together. Here the picture is defined by the reddish purple loosestrife, white iris, and reeds *(Miscanthus)*. The large-leaved pipe vine provides an attractive background.

An Exciting Arrangement

Large wooden tubs or half barrels (with a pond lining insert) can be good-looking water garden containers. The tubs are the trump cards in this arrangement. They make possible an out-of-the-ordinary deck planting that skillfully unites exotic plants with native moisture-loving perennials. Such combinations are best taken as inspiration to develop a similar construction with more common species. Mad-dog weed, pickerel weed, or a large sweet flag *(Acorus calamus)*, for example, could replace the attractive but cold-sensitive *Thalia dealbata* in the center tub. The bamboos (left rear) make a beautiful backdrop for the flower candles of the purple loosestrife and the yellow blossoms of the buttercup. The flower color and forms of the purple loosestrife are smartly picked up and varied: once with the slender ears of the giant hyssop *(Agastache,* right), again with the low-growing orchid primula *(Primula vialii,* left front). The yellow of the potentilla (right) underlines the purple and red flowers.

EXPERT TIP
Purple loosestrife can be very invasive in wetlands. Keep plants in containers.

EXPERT TIP
Most swamp perennials are easy to care for.

CROSS-REFERENCE
Planting Water Gardens pages 34–35

Delights for the Palate and Feasts for the Eyes

Information in Brief

Ornamental Flowers

Apples, pears, plums (white-pink)
Strawberries (white)
Zucchini, pumpkin (yellow, white)
Scarlet runner beans (red, white)
Borage, sage, rosemary (blue, violet)
Thyme, oregano, chives (pink, lavender)

Ornamental Fruits

Tomatoes (red, yellow)
Peppers (green, red, yellow)
Zucchini, pumpkin (green-yellow, yellow)
Eggplant (dark purple)
All fruit varieties

Ornamental Leaves/Stems

Red-stemmed chard
Herbs, especially the colored-leaf varieties (green-white, green-yellow, reddish, blue-gray)

Attractive Vines

Scarlet runner beans
Kiwi

A Country-Style Deck
Wooden railings and flooring provide the appropriate framework for a wooden box, into which is sunk a plastic box containing leaf lettuce. The corn (right) in the terra-cotta pot can hold its own with any ornamental-leaved plant and is underplanted with yellow and red bush tomatoes. Other eye-catchers: a currant bush trained as a standard and yellow marigolds (*Tagetes tenuifolia*).

Mediterranean Herb Collection
Arranged to conserve space and appeal to the eye: basil, oregano, sage, and rosemary on a corner plant stand. When situated in as sunny a spot as possible, such an arrangement rewards with an intensely agreeable fragrance and a never-ending supply of fresh herbs for the kitchen. The different leaf forms and colors are also a treat for the eyes. Bougainvillea and dark-red pinks beautifully complete the picture.

Interesting possibilities are created when the colors and shapes of vegetables, herbs, and fruit are deliberately integrated into the design.

Decorative Growth Forms

The "Collonade" apple, a columnar-form dwarf type, grown without side branches, always provides a pretty picture, even when the fruits are (still) green. The numerous herbs (lemon balm, thyme, savory, dill, marjoram, sage) grown so close by keep many a fruit pest away with their pungent fragrances. This example shows, too, how attractive the different growth forms and leaf colors of the herbs can look when they are skillfully arranged. The flowers of the nasturtiums and borage provide spots of color.

Good Enough to Eat

Anyone who likes to eat tomatoes can fall back on many different varieties for the deck. Yellow-fruited varieties such as the cherry tomato 'Sun Gold' (with a rather sweet flavor) offer a beautiful sight and contrast charmingly with red varieties, here seen as low-growing bush tomatoes. Basil is not only a good partner for tomatoes in the kitchen but also on the deck; it appears on this deck in herb baskets as small-leaved green and as bronze-leaved varieties ('Purple Ruffles'), together with sage and one of the dwarf deck tomatoes.

Tucked Away Behind Beans

Scarlet runner beans are outstanding annual climbers that quickly create privacy or shade wherever needed. As early as June they bear red or white flowers, with podded fruits by the end of July. In addition, there is the promise of the kohlrabi harvest from the deck railing and the tasty chard in the boxes on the floor. The pretty red dahlias are "merely" for decoration.

EXPERT TIP
Another yellow tomato: 'Sweet Tangerine'

CROSS-REFERENCE
Herbs, Vegetables, Fruit pages 110–119

Plant Combinations

**Playing with color and shape is fun.
Its elements are finding inspiration everywhere, trying out
your own ideas, and gathering experiences.**

One of the best avenues to having a beautiful deck is "stealing" with your eyes. You can find planting ideas everywhere—in this book, other books, garden magazines, or on someone else's deck—that, with slight changes, you can translate to your own deck at home.

Design Examples

The suggestions on the following pages are mainly oriented toward medium to small, "mobile" gardens. Transposing them to large-scale patios is certainly no problem, and for the most part they can be at least partially realized on your own minideck. Besides color harmony, the coordination of growth heights and forms plays a great role in the effect created by a planting. Axioms and guidelines always remain very abstract, however. Instead, the examples in this chapter are chosen to demonstrate visually and almost hands-on the principles of "designing."

Working Together

Varying plant characteristics and needs keep the possibilities for combinations in one plant container within more or less narrow confines:

▶ For example, vigorous, very competitive plants can overwhelm more delicate plants.

▶ Combine extremely thirsty species and those loving dryness in one box or pot—and supplying the correct amount of water for the plants becomes a game of chance.

▶ It's the same story with widely different nutrient needs. In such cases it's better to put the plants in separate containers—then groupings by preference are possible. You can either stand the individual containers separately or group them together in one deck box or a larger planter. Also, make use of the commercially available plant racks, steps and stands, hanging baskets, and strawberry planters. This permits many different kinds of arrangements with good use of space.

*A deck with a simply masterful planting:
such mastery, even of design, is not
innate, but must be learned.*

Using Color Effectively

As has already been stated: Whatever pleases you is allowed. Still, some tried and true color "laws" and principles make it easier to coordinate colors and assemble attractive, impressive plantings.

Effects of Flower Colors
In general:

▶ Yellow creates a cheerful mood and develops good glow power against dark backgrounds.

▶ Red and orange act as signals and establish clear, sometimes even explosive accents.

▶ Pink, depending on whether it is in the red, white, or blue area, presents as warm-cheerful, soft and delicate, or cool-dignified.

▶ Blue is considered the definitely "cool" color, with an elegant, even calming effect. Blue is good for creating visual depth, but it is not so effective in front of a dark background.

▶ Violet is similar in its mood to blue, but the red component provides for a warmer character.

▶ White moderates among the various color hues and brightens dark corners. But it needs other colors next to it—it might even be a vigorous leaf green—to make it truly display its powers of illumination.

These principal color effects are obviously diluted or modified when it is a matter of lighter nuances or in-between shades.

Compelling Color Combinations
The color wheel helps to give a good overview of color gradations and transitions and at the same time provides an outstanding tool for combining colors. You will find it—represented graphically as "flower colors"—on the back endpapers of this book. The different color combination principles are also demonstrated there with specific examples.

▶ Tone-on-tone describes arrangements that combine different flowers of one color, such as an "explosive red" box with geraniums (pelargoniums), petunias, and hanging verbenas. These arrangements are often varied by using deeper and lighter values of the basic color. When various mixed values are then added, you are well on your way to a color

Brilliant Yellows
Yellow flowers work like captive sunshine, looking cheerful and happy. The glowing colors of the sunflowers and marigolds contrast beautifully with the blue flower box.

scale (combinations of neighboring colors).

▶ Contrasts of complementary colors, which lie opposite each other on the color wheel, are very striking. Simply lay a ruler or other straight edge across the colored flowers and turn it—using the brown center as the pivot point—in whichever direction you want, and you will find a number of exciting combinations.

▶ A color triangle occurs when you mentally draw a triangle in the color wheel whose points then "point to" the colors that go together. Leaving out shades of green—that is, the colors of leaves—you inevitably come to the time-tested basic color combinations of yellow-red-blue and their variants. White, as a neutral "noncolor," is outside the color wheel and can be combined in almost any way desired. White plus bright yellow, or with other very light colors, however, often looks simply washed out. Two basic ways to use white effectively:

▶ Add white flowers to colored ones, which creates a complementary contrast.

▶ Substitute white for one of the three colors in a color triangle. For example, white-red-blue is a very beautiful combination with its own special ambience.

Foliage plants in various green shades, leaf forms, and leaf sizes can also be used to design beautiful combinations.

Styles and Moods

The effects of the individual colors listed above give an indication of what moods the different combinations convey.

▶ A cheerful, even brilliant picture is achieved by large proportions of yellow, orange, and red. But the most cheerful feelings can be "dashed" by such arrangements if the eye cannot find a resting place. Especially on a small deck, too much colorful exuberance can become tiring over time. White and green (foliage plants) provide resting places.

▶ White, blue, purple, and pink, and also pastel tints, create a "romantic," delicate-lively, or even dignified basic mood. In a narrow space it is often advantageous to have gentle hues dominate. Using blue and white predominantly can even make a small deck appear larger.

▶ The interplay between color and form is very close. Large, striking flowers embody the color effects and moods very assertively; just think of the unambiguous brilliance of red begonias or the distinctly "noble" blue-violet petunia flowers. Delicate flowers, even if the plants are luxuriantly covered with them, always appear somewhat looser and more playful, even when the colors of the flowers are explosive.

Planting Ideas for Spring

Information in Brief

Planting Suggestions

Saucer planter (16 in. [40 cm] Ø):
    16 crocuses of mixed
    colors, 12 snowdrops,
    9 yellow narcissi 'Tête-à-
    Tête', 9 red tulips

Saucer planter (12 in. [30 cm] Ø):
    3 white hyacinths, 15 blue
    grape hyacinths, 2 purple
    primulas, 2 pink English
    daisies

Saucer planter (12 in. [30 cm] Ø):
    9 white tulips, 4 blue hya-
    cinths, 5 yellow violas

Box (24 in. [60 cm] long):
    6 red-yellow tulips, 9 white
    miniature narcissi, 2 red and
    1 yellow primula

Box (32 in. [80 cm] long):
    6 red-white tulips, 3 yellow
    wallflowers, 3 forget-me-nots,
    3 yellow pansies

Box (39 in. [100 cm] long):
    2 red-leaved bergenias,
    12 yellow narcissi, 5 blue
    violas

Romantic Spring Deck

An enchanting spring idyll, which here gains its special effect from the symmetrical basic structure: two trailing pussy willows, posted in the corners, frame the front of the deck. The "pairing principle" is continued by the two dwarf cherries (*Prunus serrulata*, special small forms) and underlined once more by the two boxwoods in tubs. Were it only a matter of large-leaved compact plants with strong flower colors, the arrangement would look almost boring; however, it is just the opposite with the preponderance of loose growth forms and the delicate shades of the tulips. Restrained red and violet flowers (pansies, English daisies, primulas) as well as the yellow dwarf forsythia round out the picture.

Forced bulbs bought in spring allow dense plantings. However, greenhouse-raised plants are very frost-sensitive.

Mood: Refined to Cheerful

A 24-in. (60-cm) box with 9 white narcissi 'Flower Record', 9 yellow narcissi 'Limerick', 9 hyacinths; on each of the long sides, 1 grape hyacinth, 3 blue and white primulas, 2 yellow pansies. For fall planting, set out only 5–7 each of narcissi and hyacinths.

Strong Spring Signals

A 32-in. (80-cm) box with yellow-red, red, and white botanical tulips, in groups of 5 each; in between, 3 wallflowers, along the edge of the box 3 primulas and 2 violet pansies.

Delicate Spring Greeting

In spite of its restrained flower colors, this attractive pot planting is hardly unnoticeable: 5 tulips, 3 each of English daisies, forget-me-nots, and grape hyacinths, crowned by 3 enchanting bleeding-hearts (*Dicentra spectabilis*) deck the handsome container. When such decorative containers have no drainage hole, you should use them just as cachepots and actually plant the plants in plastic pots of the appropriate size.

Brilliant Show of Color

Here the grouping of plants in individual pots and the "airy" arrangement on the corner plant stand make the strong colors of the flowers show to especially good effect. The narcissi, pansies, tulips, and hyacinths form the classic color triangle of yellow-red-blue/violet. The azalea (pictured top right) contributes still another strong red variant.

EXPERT TIP
Bleeding-hearts bloom from April to May; they prefer part shade.

CROSS-REFERENCE
Spring Flowers pages 58–61

Planting Ideas for Summer

Information in Brief

Summer-Flowering Potted Perennials

For sunny locations:
Delphinium (*Delphinium* hybrids), blue flowers
Gay-feather (*Liatris spicata* 'Kobold'), violet
Catmint (*Nepeta* x *faassenii*), lavender blue
Coneflower (*Rudbeckia nitida*), yellow

For sun and part shade:
Columbine (*Aquilegia* species), blue
Cranesbill (*Geranium* species), pink, red, violet
Day lilies (*Hemerocallis* hybrids), yellow, orange, red
Coral bells (*Heuchera* species), pink, red
Bee Balm (*Monarda* hybrids), red, pink, lavender

For shady locations:
Lady's mantle (*Alchemilla mollis*), yellow-green
Astilbe (*Astilbe* species), red, pink, white
Hosta (*Hosta* species), white, lavender

Lushly Colorful Congregation of Flowers

Green and blooming on all levels: At the top, the trailing scaevola and climbing morning glory join in a violet tone-on-tone combination. The white of the argyranthemum leads down to the gay flower arrangement on the floor level. Delphinium, sunflowers, marigolds, and lobelias are placed next to each other in bedlike arrangement by height. When making such intensive use of space, bear in mind that each plant must remain easily accessible for watering and maintenance jobs.

Queen and Court

The rose is known as "queen of the flowers" and is represented here by 'Iceberg' (up to 48 in. [1.2 m] tall). Just as noble in appearance is the lily, whose orange color harmonizes beautifully with its blue companions: lavender, campanula, cat mint (right front), and delphinium (in background). These are typical companions for roses in the garden, as are the yellow rudbeckias. They will also last well in pots for at least one season. Very important for roses and perennials: a drainage layer (gravel, perlite) at the bottom of the pot.

Low-growing varieties of many garden perennials can also be cultivated in pots, enriching the deck plant repertoire.

Summer Dream in a Box

This deck box is a treasure to rivet all eyes the whole summer long. Slender salvias (*Salvia farinacea*) in bluish purple and white form the background. A verbena (*Verbena* hybrid) is planted at each end as a trailing counterpoint. In the center is the golden yellow tickseed (*Coreopsis*), effectively underpainted by dark purple cupflowers (*Nierembergia*) and lobelia. A light pink standard rose (left) and wax begonias in a pot offer discreet support.

Nordic Flair

Blue-white hues, combined with warm yellow: This is a color combination common to Scandinavian countries. To visually "cool down" warm summers, you should try out this Nordic principle, which also distinguishes "Summer Dream in a Box" (see illustration at left): Brilliant yellow flowers are sparingly planted between colors with predominantly cool effects as striking accents. In this example they are sunflowers and marigolds. White plants: cascade petunias, argyranthemums. Violet/blue: two morning glories, scaeveola (hanging pot), and delphinium.

Beautiful in the Shade

A 32-in. (80-cm) box with 3 red tuberous-rooted begonias, 2 bright-violet impatiens (*Impatiens New Guinea* hybrids), and 3 trailing fuchsias at the edge of the box. Beautiful variations are possible using yellow begonias, white impatiens, or an upright white-and-blue fuchsia (in center of the box).

Splendid in the Sun

A 32-in. (80-cm) box: 4 dark red tobacco plants 'Nicki Red', 1 yellow argyranthemum 'Butterfly', 2 blue-and-white verbenas, 2 white and 1 blue lobelia.

EXPERT TIP
White petunias, with their large flowers, are optimal "lighteners."

CROSS-REFERENCE
Summer Flowers pages 64–81

Planting Ideas for Fall and Winter

Information in Brief

Potted Shrubs with Fall Color

Attractive foliage:

> Dwarf Japanese maple (*Acer palmatum dissectum*)
>
> Fern leaf maple (*Acer japonicum* 'Aconitifolium')
>
> Barberry (*Berberis thunbergii*); also ornamental fruits
>
> Burning bush (*Euonymus alatus*)
>
> Virginia creeper (*Parthenocissus quinquefolia*)
>
> Japanese flowering cherry (*Prunus serrulata*)
>
> Staghorn sumac (*Rhus typhina*)

Ornamental fruits:

> Cotoneaster (*Cotoneaster dammeri, C. x Watereri* hybrids)
>
> Firethorn (*Pyracantha* hybrids 'Soleil d'Or', 'Golden Charmer')
>
> Japanese skimmia (*Skimmia japonica*)
>
> Pernettya (*Pernettya mucronata*)

Glowing Color Until Frost

Sturdy golden yellow chrysanthemums ward off any fall depression whatsoever. The red dahlias with yellow centers are wonderful partners with comparable illuminating powers. Discreet companions: light-pink potted heath (*Erica gracilis*), green-yellow grassy-leaved sweet flag (*Acorus gramineus*), and silvery common groundsel. In a sheltered spot (cover with floating row cover before night frosts), the glorious bloom can be kept going into November.

The Colors of Fall

The magic of the gradual change in leaf colors—only fall has this to offer. The jeweled berries of the dwarf cotoneaster standard glow against the red autumn garb of the grape vines and the sweet gum (*Liquidambar styraciflua*)—as an evergreen, it also holds the fort during the winter season.

Also make use in fall plantings of the multitude of ornamental-leaved plants, such as variegated ajuga and silvery santolina.

Late-Season Romantic

This can be a good place to sit on mild fall days: The delicate shades of potted heaths, fall chrysanthemums, and asters generate an excited-cheerful mood. The heaths' varietal spectrum, which consists chiefly of all different shades of pink, along with white and crimson, make them just exactly right for a tone-on-tone planting. Appropriate chrysanthemum and aster varieties are not hard to find. The pot heath (*Erica gracilis*) blooms especially richly, but in contrast to the Scotch heather and alpine heath, it is not winter hardy.

Winter—So What?

Now let the cold season come! The long-lasting berries of the firethorn (*Pyracantha* hybrids) aren't scared off by a little frost or the first snowflakes; no more is the Scotch heather, which blooms all the way into December, depending on the variety. But the ones with the more impressively ornamental leaves are the white-edged ivy and the ajuga (*Ajuga reptans*), with the reddish cast of its leaves. It is advisable to wrap the pot for protection when there is threat of severe frost.

Decorative All Year-Long

A box 24 in. (60 cm) with Scotch pine (*Pinus sylvestris* 'Watereri'), on the right a dwarf pine (*Pinus mugo* var. *pumilio*), on the left deciduous bar-berry (*Berberis thunbergii*, with red fall color) and skimmia. Augment with seasonally appropriate flowers—here, in a summer example, wax begonias and white asters.

Winter Decoration

A box 24 in. (60 cm) with yellow Japanese falsecypress (*Chamaecyparis pisifera* 'Plumosa aurea'), Scotch heather, and dwarf Bosnian pine (*Pinus leucodermis*). In the fall, plant flowering bulbs in between.

EXPERT TIP
Water all evergreens occasionally when temperature is above freezing.

CROSS-REFERENCE
Ornamental Shrubs pages 88–97

Fragrant Combinations

Information in Brief

Fragrances for Deck and Terrace

Flower-fresh smell:
  Scented geranium
  (*Pelargonium graveolens*)
  Common mignonette (*Reseda odorata*)
  Sweet violet (*Viola odorata*)

Spicy smell:
  Lavender cotton (*Santolina*)
  Herbs

Lemony smell:
  Lemon verbena (*Aloysia triphylla*)
  Lemon balm (*Melissa officinalis*)
  Scented geranium
  (*Pelargonium crispum, P. citronella*)

Evening scented:
  Angel's trumpets (*Datura, Brugmansia*)
  Stock (*Matthiola incana*)
  Four-o'clock (*Mirabilis jalapa*)

Aromatic insect repellers:
  Swedish ivy (*Plectranthus*)
  Common rue (*Ruta graveolens*)
  Tomatoes

Competition of Good Smells

A deck for epicures: The lilies to the left and right of the chair smell especially intense in the evening, as does the collection of tobacco plants in the boxes. During the day 'Wave' petunias (in the hanging pots) and sweet peas pamper the nose with their sweet, flowery scent, while the Russian sage with its light-blue flower candles is somewhat spicier. An especially lovely perfume is that of the star jasmine (at left), a hothouse plant with twining shoots and little white flowers. There are scented geraniums (right front) with various fragrance notes—according to the species— from rose to bracing balsam. Like most fragrant-leaved plants, scented geraniums give off their good smell when they are touched. They bloom much less than other geraniums, and in fact the best fragrance plants are often rather inconspicuous.

It is advisable to choose fragrant partners for combination rather sparingly and cautiously at first—and, of course, always according to your nose.

Vivacious and Fragrant

In aromatherapy, fragrances are combined with yellow and a shot of purple to diminish stress. Try it yourself—cheerful yellow puts people in a more or less happy mood. Planting: deck boxes with lavender cotton (*Santolina chamaecyparis*), calendulas, and nasturtiums (1); marigolds (*Tagetes tenuifolia*) in pots (2); bright yellow lemon balm (variety 'Variegata') (3) and nasturtiums (4); hanging pot with moneywort 'Lyssi' (5). The purple accent is provided by a heliotrope (6), which smells especially intense in the evening.

Flowery, Spicy, Fresh

The fragrant hanging basket (1) is planted with 4 marigolds (*Tagetes tenuifolia*), 3 scented geraniums (*Pelargonium odoratissimum*), 2 'Wave' petunias, and 2 variegated sages (*Salvia officinalis* 'Tricolor'). Growing in the tub is the intoxicatingly fragrant rose 'Margaret Merril' (up to 32 in. [80 cm] tall), underplanted with marigolds and sweet alyssum (2). You can, of course, place the rose and the fragrant hanging basket in different spots on the deck if the potpourri of aromas gets to be too much for you. The sweet peas (3) contribute a delicate scent.

For Night Owls

"Moon plants" don't give off their perfumes until evening—just the right thing for soft summer nights. Climbing scented backdrop: an evergreen honeysuckle (*Lonicera henryi*) (1). White and red flowering tobacco with sweet alyssum (2) as well as stocks (3) grace the deck boxes. The white flowers work their effect—faintly luminous—even in the dark. All plants tolerate part shade during the day. Heavy, sweet scents can be overpowering in excess, so it's advisable to do a "smell test" with the honeysuckle, especially, before installing it on the deck.

EXPERT TIP
Look for heat-resistant and fragrant sweet pea varieties.

CROSS-REFERENCE
Scents of Provence page 145

A Touch of the Mediterranean

Information in Brief

Mediterranean Hothouse Plants

Agave (*Agave americana*)
Bougainvillea (*Bougainvillea*)
European fan palm (*Chamaerops humilis*)
Laudanum (*Cistus ladanifer*)
Citrus trees (*Citrus*)
Fig tree (*Ficus carica*)
Bay laurel (*Laurus nobilis*)
Myrtle (*Myrtus communis*)
Oleander (*Nerium oleander*)
Olive (*Olea europea*)
Laurustinus (*Viburnum tinus*)

Appropriate Annuals

Snapdragon (*Antirrhinum majus*)
Asteriscus (*Asteriscus maritimus*)
Pot marigold (*Calendula officinalis*)
Fleabane (*Erigeron* x *hybridus*)
Marguerite Daisy (*Chrysanthemum frutescens*)
Sweet pea (*Lathryus odoratus*)
Sweet alyssum (*Lobularia maritima*)
Ice plant (*Mesembryanthemum criniflorum*)
Geranium (*Pelargonium*)
Portulaca (*Portulaca grandiflora*)

Mediterranean Potpourri

Vacation "in Deckland" or "on Patio Island"—why not? Our design example mixes elements of different Mediterranean countries. The blue-and-white interior is reminiscent of so many Greek or Spanish building facades. The pink flowers of the fragrant laudanum (*Cistus ladanifer*) (2) go beautifully with it as does the little bay laurel tree (6) as doorkeeper. Lavender, rosemary, sage, tomatoes, basil, and arugula in pots and boxes (4) offer "southland" for the eyes, nose, and taste. The grape vine (1) in the planter needs about 4 years to cover the trellis attractively (a large tub and good winter protection required). The boxes (3) hold geraniums, argyranthemums, asteriscus, and flea-bane; *Convolvulus sabatica* is growing in the hanging pot (5).

**Provided there's enough sun, a wealth of
typical "vacation plants" will also thrive in planters and
pots on decks and patios in northern climes.**

Scents of Provence

The effect of endless blue fields of lavender can scarcely be reproduced on the deck, but even in pots *Lavandula angustifolia* is an ornament. Besides blue there are also white varieties; they start blooming in June and often keep going all summer long. Lavender needs little water; it is wintered over frost free and bright or outside with winter protection. Here thyme and oregano are installed in the deck boxes as aromatic companions. The bay laurel standard fits very well into the Provencal-flavored scenario, as does the grape vine (right).

Indispensables: Hothouse Plants

Besides South America, Africa, and Asia, a great variety of hothouse plants also come from the Mediterranean region. A dwarf orange tree and a bougainvillea, here as an exquisite standard, can provide a Mediterranean ambience. And if you don't have quite enough space for a grove of cypresses, the attractive Monterey cypress (*Cupressus macrocarpa* 'Goldcrest') should fill the bill. It thrives best when it is placed outside in the summer and wintered over cool inside. On the trellis: a passion flower.

Characteristic Forms

The opposite side of the deck in the middle picture is also made consistent with the "southern" design with the aid of typical growth and leaf forms. The highlight is the large fig tree, beside which a small pine is growing in a pot. The interesting white-yellow-red flowers belong to the star-glory vine (*Quamoclit pinnata*), an annual twining plant. White trellises and railings as well as the basket chair go very well with the ambience of this planting.

EXPERT TIP
Terra-cotta containers are the first choice for the Mediterranean deck.

CROSS-REFERENCE
Hothouse Plants pages 98–109

A Place for Children

Information in Brief

Not Safe for Small Children

Very poisonous plants:

- Boxwood (*Buxus sempervirens*)
- Autumn crocus (*Colchicum autumnale*)
- Cotoneaster (*Cotoneaster*)
- Daphne (*Daphne*)
- Angel's trumpets (*Datura, Brugmansia*)
- Ivy (*Hedera helix*)
- Honeysuckle (*Lonicera*)
- Narcissi (*Narcissus*)
- Oleander (*Nerium oleander*)
- Tobacco plant (*Nicotiana*)
- Cherry laurel (*Prunus laurocerasus*)
- Rhododendron, azalea (*Rhododendron*)
- Blue potato bush (*Solanum rantonnetii*)
- Yew (*Taxus*)
- Arborvitae (*Thuja*)

Prickery, thorny plants:

- Agave (*Agave americana*)
- Barberry (*Berberis*)
- European fan palm (*Chamaerops humilis*)
- Firethorn (*Pyracantha coccinea*)
- Roses (*Rosa*)

Children's Paradise—Small, but Nice

A deck needn't be very large for a play area like this. With portable or collapsible furniture, it can even be set up quickly and cleared away again in the evening, when the grown-ups want to sit at their deck table, for instance. However, at the critical age between "mobile-adventure-seeking" and "not quite able to reason yet" nothing should be placed near the deck railings that could inspire risky clambering explorations on the balustrade.

Besides all kinds of playthings, there are colorful plantings and decorations like the windmills here to make children feel comfortable on the deck. During the noonday heat they can play quite comfortably and without any risk of sunburn under the improvised sunshade. At the same time, with very simple means, it provides the secret-fort atmosphere that many children love.

With folding chairs and planters or plant shelves on wheels, a somewhat more open play area can quickly be created.

Avoiding Risks

With small children, safety is the number one priority. Caution: Many tropical and deck plants are more or less poisonous; check with the warning notes in the plant portraits section. Also, it's better to avoid plants with prickers or thorns on a children's deck. Where the "holey" railings can't be made child-safe by fastening wooden boards over them, a good firm wire netting will help, which can be planted with pharbitis (1), for example, and black-eyed Susans (2). A toy-chest-bench for stowing away playthings is a practical feature.

A Deck Learning Space

For children over the age of 5, the deck can become a small "learning space," with brightly colored snapdragons (1), sunflowers (2), a yardstick for measuring growth, and a weathervane that shows which way the wind is blowing. It's fun for them to make their own deck decorations, for instance a mobile with flower or animal themes. And perhaps it will also be for you: Fragrances are part of the most intense childhood memories. Herbs (3) provide for stimulating scent experiences; the four o'clock (*Mirabilis jalapa*) (4) doesn't open its fragrant, varicolored flowers until late afternoon.

A Child's Very Own Garden

Somewhat bigger children become enthusiastic about gardening. The first home-grown flower is always a special thrill! The best plants for this purpose are ones that grow well in boxes with direct sowing, especially nasturtiums (1) and pot marigolds and sweet peas (2). The same goes for radishes, if vegetables are desired. When it comes to taking care of "their own" tomatoes (3) or strawberries (4), children are especially diligent—at least temporarily.

Nature at the Window

Information in Brief

Annuals/Summer Flowers

Pheasant's eye (*Adonis aestivalis*), blood red, poisonous!

Corn cockle (*Agrostemma githago*), red-purple, poisonous!

Scarlet pimpernel (*Anagallis arvensis*), red

Bachelor's button, cornflower (*Centaurea cyanis*), blue, pink

Larkspur (*Consolida regalis*), blue, poisonous!

California poppy (*Eschscholzia californica*), yellow, orange, white

Love-in-a-mist (*Nigella damascena*), blue, pink, white

Corn poppy (*Papaver rhoeas*), red

Naturalizing Perennials

Columbine (*Aquilegia vulgaris*), blue, poisonous!

Golden marguerites (*Anthemis tinctoria*), yellow

Pinks (*Dianthus deltoides*), crimson

Common foxglove (*Digitalis purpurea*), red, poisonous!

Inula (*Inula ensifolia*), yellow

Betony (*Stachys officinalis*), bluish purple

Wild Charm

Selecting plants that offer abundant food for hummingbirds, butterflies, and other insects will help create a more natural and interesting deck ambience. The deck boxes in our example are designed according to the color triangle yellow-red-blue: (2) calendulas, borage, pinks; (3) golden marguerites, larkspur, bachelor's buttons; (4) inula, bachelor's buttons, pinks. On the trellis (1): *Clematis alpina*. On the herb stand (5): dwarf houseleek, sage, dill, thyme. A shadbush is growing in the large planter (6). Plants on the right, shady side of the deck (7): columbine, foxglove, campanulas, dead nettle; in front of them, wild strawberries (8) and ferns (9). This little-used corner is also the best location for a bird feeder. Most of the plants used are perennials and can be wintered over outside. Provide wild plants with organic fertilizer if possible: Feed the annuals monthly, the perennials only every other spring.

On the natural deck, the object is not spectacular bloom:
The plants obtain their effects through their charm—
in fact, through their naturalness.

Delicate Shades

The effect of this "wild company" in the beautiful plant jar is utterly enchanting. You could also include Butterfly weed (*Asclepias tuberosa*), Purple coneflower (*Echinacea purpurea*), Sunflowers (*Helianthus* spp.), Switch grass (*Panicum virgatum*), painted tongues (*Salpiglossis sinuata*), and the yellow evening primroses (*Oenothera biennis*) to further attract birds and butterflies to your deck. The primrose is a good food plant for moths.

Wildflowers in Deck Boxes

Bachelor's buttons, corn cockles, California bluebells (*Phacelia*), daisies, corn poppies—you can have the entire glory of the flowering meadow on the deck. Flower seed mixtures designed especially for boxes are becoming increasingly available, but you can also use annual meadow flower mixtures. Sowing is done in March/April, preferably in seed mix or unfertilized garden soil. Just press the seeds in and cover lightly with soil.

Vibrant Summer Colors

The use of pot marigolds and bachelor's buttons in this pleasing summer box provides a striking color contrast. Both species can be raised first and then put together or be sown directly in the box. The latter produces the most natural effect; with the use of grown plants, on the other hand, the colors and the growth heights can be set off against one another to the best advantage. In this example, the front planting of a trailing variety of evening primrose (*Oenothera*) is a charming touch.

EXPERT TIP
Low-growing wildflower seed mixtures work well in containers.

Explantion of Technical Terms

Some of the technical terms used in the text may not be familiar to everyone and are thus explained here.

Annuals: "Real" annual plants bloom in the year of sowing and, if they are allowed to, produce fruit (develop seeds) and then die. This category includes many vegetables and herbs, as well as numerous summer flowers. But among deck flowers there are also shrubs or subshrubs that are only raised as annuals. This is because with maintenance in boxes, or rather, under our climatic conditions, the next year's new growth develops poorly.

Biennials: A plant that lives for two years or two growing seasons. These plants produce flowers and seed in the second year and then die, for example, pansies, English daisies, forget-me-nots, parsley.

Bloom: Flowers, the totality of the flowers. In some plants, a main phase of bloom and a somewhat weaker second bloom can be clearly determined.

Conifers: "Cone bearers," that is, all needle-leaved woody plants that—usually after some years—develop cones, such as spruce and pine. Junipers and yews do not belong to this group, since instead of cones they develop berrylike fruits.

Container plants: Young plants that were raised in the nursery in plastic pots or wrappers. Advantages: more compact root balls, can be planted almost any time of year (even when flowering), are already used to life in a pot.

Cuttings: Growth tissue that after being cut off from the mother plant will root and from which new, complete plants will grow. We distinguish between tip cuttings (ends of growing shoots) and stem cuttings (from the middle of the shoot); there are also leaf and root cuttings.

Double flowers: In single flowers (e.g., the wild rose), only one circle of petals surrounds the stamens and pistil. In double flowers (e.g., the hybrid tea rose), there are more petals in addition to those; depending on the number of petals, the flowers are known as semidouble or very double.

Geraniums: Widely used term for pelargoniums, which is, strictly speaking, incorrect. In the beginning, the plants that have been so popular for hundreds of years were thought to be related to the cranesbill (genus *Geranium*), but they have been classified botanically in the genus *Pelargonium* since 1789.

Late frosts: The days between May 12 and 15, known as the Ice Saints in some regions after the calendar saints' days for Pancratius, Servatius, Boniface, and Sophia. During this period in the olden days night frosts

would still very often occur. According to weather statistics this is rarely the case—depending on the region; nevertheless the day "after the ice saints" has become the tag line for moving boxes and hothouse plants outside. Also in the last third of the month (from May 20) cool, raw storms come up, which must be heeded, especially in the case of sensitive plants.

Part-shade: Describes a plant location that either is in the shade for about half the day or is only lightly shaded the entire day.

Perennials: Plants that live many years and are herbaceous (not woody); thanks to long-lived roots or rootstock (rhizome) they continue to put out new growth after a resting period—usually winter. Bulbs and corms also are perennials in the botanical meaning of the word.

pH Value: Unit of measure for the degree of acidity of soil or water, which can be determined by using pH kits available from a garden center or nursery supplier. A pH value of 7 is neutral, values under that indicate acid milieu, and with values over 7 (up to 14) we speak of basic or alkaline. High pH values indicate a high lime content; lime-sensitive plants like azaleas thrive only in acid soils.

Softwood cuttings: Slightly woody cuttings, whose bark is still not quite hardened. In some woody plants and tropicals, it is the optimal stage for taking cuttings.

Soilless mix: In the garden trade these are mixtures of peat, loam, humus, vermiculite, and perlite that are used for container plants and for propagating plants.

Subshrubs: Perennial plants in which the lower stems become woody over time, but the upper ones, on the other hand, remain herbaceous.

Succulents: Plants that can store water in their thick, fleshy leaves, which indicates origins in dry, desertlike regions. Examples: agave, crassula.

Species, Varieties, Hybrids

Species are the "plants as such"; example: garden crocus (*Crocus vernus*) and deck crocus (*Crocus chrysanthus*) are two different species of the genus *Crocus*. The uncapitalized Latin (botanical) name gives the precise species description, and in case of any doubt, it is clearer than the common English name: for example, *Crocus chrysanthus* also means "colored crocus."

Varieties are vegetatively bred plant species and often have fanciful names, which are enclosed in single quotation marks. Examples: *Crocus vernus* 'Remembrance' designates a dark purple garden crocus variety, 'Jeanne d'Arc' a pure white one. Varieties can differ not only in the color of the flower but also in the growth height and form, even in their tolerance for shade.

Hybrids are seed produced from cross fertilizing two different plant varieties. The first generation of plants of the resulting seed is referred to as the F_1 hybrids. Seed collected and grown from F_1 hybrids are called F_2 hybrids and will not have the same characteristics as the F_1 hybrids.

Resources

Plant and Garden Supply Catalogs

Alberta Nurseries & Seed Co.
P.O. Box 20
Bowden, Alberta
Canada TOM OKO
(403) 224-3544
plants, seeds, and supplies

Bluestone Perennials
7211 Middle Ridge Road
Madison, OH 44057
800-852-5243
extensive perennial and biennial selection

W. Atlee Burpee
300 Park Avenue
Warminster, PA 18974
800-888-1447
www.burpee.com
seeds, plants, and gardening supplies

D. V. Burrell Seed Growers Co.
P.O. Box 150
Rocky Ford, CO 81067-0150
(719) 254-3318
seeds, books, supplies, and tools

Gardener's Supply Company
128 Intervale Road
Burlington, VT 05401
888-833-1412
www.gardeners.com
indoor and outdoor gardening supplies

Johnny's Selected Seeds
Foss Hill Road
Albion, ME 04910
(207) 437-9294
www.johnnyseeds.com
seeds, plants, and gardening supplies

Lilypons Water Garden
P.O. Box 10
Buckeystown, MD 21717
800-723-7667
www.lilypons.com
full selection of water plants and water gardening supplies

Stark Bros
P.O. Box 398
Louisiana, MO 63353
(573) 754-5511
www.farmworld.com
offers a selection of dwarf fruit trees

Magazines

Fine Gardening
Taunton Press, Inc.
P.O. Box 355
South Main Street
Newton, CT 06470

Horticulture Magazine
98 North Washington Street
Boston, MA 02114-1913
800-234-2415

Organic Gardening
Rodale Press
33 East Minor Street
Emmaus, PA 18098
800-666-2206
www.organicgardening.com

Web Sites

Each site has excellent information.
www.burpee.com
www.garden-gate@prairienet.org
www.gardenguides.com
www.gardennet.com
www.gardenweb.com

County Extension Agencies

Your local county extension agency is available to help you with your gardening questions and problems and to conduct soil testing. Extension agencies are listed in the blue pages or government services section of your telephone book.

Index and Species Index

Pages with * indicate where the detailed description of the particular plant is found. The bold-faced page numbers indicate colored photographs or drawings.

Photo Credits

The photographs in this book were taken by Friedrich Strauss, with the exception of:

Floraprint/Kok: page 80 right;
Floraprint/Kooiman: page 72 left;
Henseler: pages 44, 45;
König: page 85 center;
Nickig: pages 60 center, 93 center, 112, 113 left, center;
Reinhard: pages 9 right, 36 center, bottom, 90 right, 94, 95 right, 96 right;
Sammer: page 117.

Acknowledgments

Photographer and publisher thank the garden owners and firms for their support, especially: Bärbel Speckle, Ergolding, BRD; Blattwerk, Ravensburg, BRD; Grün-Idee, Hohenthann, BRD; Die Gartengalerie, Walzbachtal, BRD.

English translation © 2002 by Barron's Educational Series, Inc.

Published originally under the title:
Balkon und Kübelpflanzen für Einsteiger
© 2000 Gräfe und Unzer Verlag GmbH. München

Translated from the German by Elizabeth D. Crawford

All rights reserved. No part of this book may be reproduced in any form, by photostat, microfilm, xerography, or any other means, or incorporated into any information retrieval system, electronic or mechanical, without the written permission of the copyright owner.

All inquiries should be addressed to:
Barron's Educational Series, Inc.
250 Wireless Boulevard
Hauppauge, New York 11788
http://www.barronseduc.com

Library of Congress Catalog Card No.
00-112042

International Standard Book No.
0-7641-5413-3

Printed in Hong Kong

9 8 7 6 5 4 3 2 1

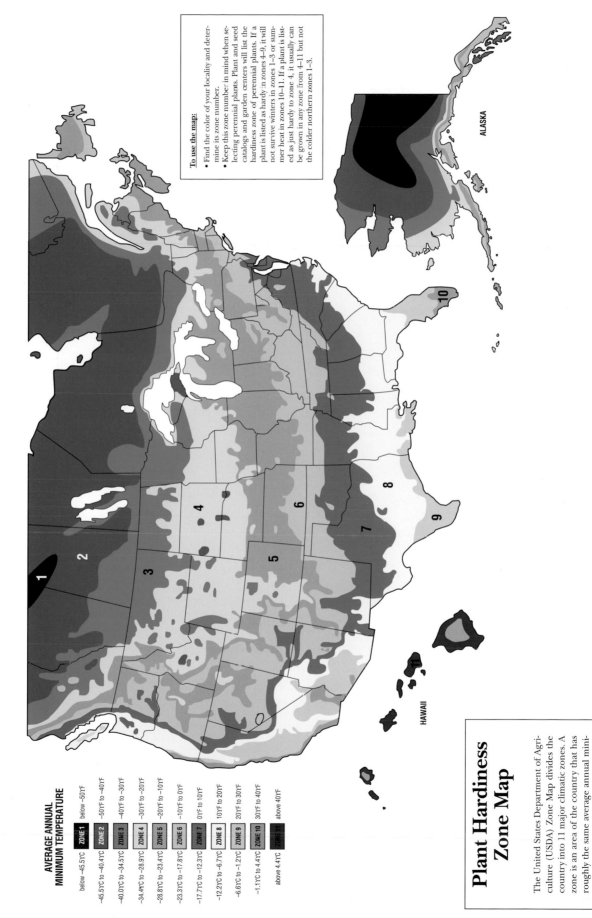

AVERAGE ANNUAL MINIMUM TEMPERATURE

ZONE 1	below −50ºF
ZONE 2	−50ºF to −40ºF
ZONE 3	−40ºF to −30ºF
ZONE 4	−30ºF to −20ºF
ZONE 5	−20ºF to −10ºF
ZONE 6	−10ºF to 0ºF
ZONE 7	0ºF to 10ºF
ZONE 8	10ºF to 20ºF
ZONE 9	20ºF to 30ºF
ZONE 10	30ºF to 40ºF
ZONE 11	above 40ºF

below −45.5ºC
−45.5ºC to −40.4ºC
−40.0ºC to −34.5ºC
−34.4ºC to −28.9ºC
−28.8ºC to −23.4ºC
−23.3ºC to −17.8ºC
−17.7ºC to −12.3ºC
−12.2ºC to −6.7ºC
−6.6ºC to −1.2ºC
−1.1ºC to 4.4ºC
above 4.4ºC

To use the map:

- Find the color of your locality and determine its zone number.
- Keep this zone number in mind when selecting perennial plants. Plant and seed catalogs and garden centers will list the hardiness zone of perennial plants. If a plant is listed as hardy in zones 4–9, it will not survive winters in zones 10–11. If a plant is listed as just hardy to zone 4, it usually can be grown in any zone from 4–11 but not the colder northern zones 1–3.

ALASKA

HAWAII

Plant Hardiness Zone Map

The United States Department of Agriculture (USDA) Zone Map divides the country into 11 major climatic zones. A zone is an area of the country that has roughly the same average annual minimum temperature.

Zone information courtesy Agricultural Research Service, USDA.

The Color Wheel as a Design Tool

Tone-on-Tone

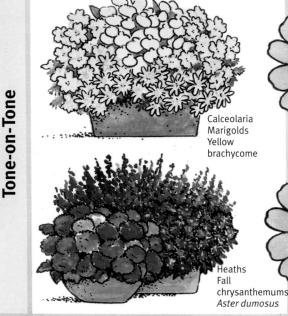

Calceolaria
Marigolds
Yellow
brachycome

Heaths
Fall
chrysanthemums
Aster dumosus

Color Scale

Potted rose
Lobelia
Lavender

Fuchsia
Tuberous-
rooted
begonias

The color wheel shows the primary colors yellow, red, and blue and their mixes arranged together, like a rainbow. Colors with less intensity or a high proportion of white have the effect of pastel tones, delicate and soft.

White

In the theory of color, white is not considered a "real" color. In practice it is outstandingly suitable as a flower color used to moderate between other colors.